The ~~Deslexic~~ ~~Dislexic~~ ~~Dixletic~~ Dyslexic Poet

Not to Mention a Great Autobiography

TOM PLATZER

ISBN 978-1-64416-001-5 (paperback)
ISBN 978-1-64416-002-2 (digital)

Copyright © 2019 by Tom Platzer

All rights reserved. No part of this publication may be reproduced, distributed, or transmitted in any form or by any means, including photocopying, recording, or other electronic or mechanical methods without the prior written permission of the publisher. For permission requests, solicit the publisher via the address below.

Christian Faith Publishing, Inc.
832 Park Avenue
Meadville, PA 16335
www.christianfaithpublishing.com

Printed in the United States of America

Acknowledgment

Mike Hafner

I was talking to my brother-in-law; he says "Tom do you have me in your book?" I said "no". His reply was, "maybe I will have to take you out of my will". I wouldn't want that to happen. He just bought a one and a half million-dollar house in Florida. He has a million-dollar home on the lake here in Minnesota, and a 52-foot boat that he says ain't big enough, and a few antique cars. I guess one could say he was a great guy. Mike has always had a big heart. I guess you could say he is a swell person. Always there to give a hand, and knows how to throw one hell-of-a-party. When you go to his party he has two bands; one croaky band and a regular band. And an open bar and all the food you can eat. I would be surprised if he left me in his will.

I just wanted to say a little word about Tom Maciejko and his sister, Mary; fine people. I worked thirty-five years with Tommy; he's the kind of guy that always that's always happy to see you and quick to buy you a drink. If you stop at Tom's house, he will invite you and make you feel comfortable---salute Tommy.

Dear diary: I ran into a deer today smash the car pretty good. The guy at the body shop said repairs would be five-grand, easily. Hey, one block from the stoplight. I had the car up to forty miles per hour. The gal that stopped to see if I was okay said the deer came out of nowhere. Fifty-two years of driving and never a scratch. Lucky, I have another car; it happened 6-21-18, at 4:00 pm in the afternoon.

Autobiography

Hi, my name Thomas Platzer. I'm going to take on this arduous task of writing this autobiography. I use the word *arduous* because it's difficult for me to transpose words in a legible manner. I love words—hey I'm a poet! I love to manipulate, twist, turn, bend, and use words, but this does not mean I can spell. I could never write in public Hand me a piece of chalk, and I start sweating. I thought I would give you some insight in to the complicated life of a learning-disabled person. Hopefully I can provide some inspiration for those like me, and maybe they can find some solace in knowing that success can be achieved through perseverance, tenacity, and belief in oneself. There is an old adage, "It's not the size of the dog in the fight, it's the size of the fight in the dog" (Mark Twain). Attitude is everything—persistence and the ability to bounce back. Like the old Timex watch, we take a licking but keep on ticking. The schooling we are exposed to will have an effect on us; it might be minuscule, but our arsenal of coping skills gets bigger. I'm saying anything that can improve your ability to understand and increase the awareness of your surroundings will add to your bottom line. Your cognitive skills will increase, thus comes the ability to see the world as a bigger place. What I learned in collage greatly outdistanced whatever I learned previously.

I believe learning disabilities are as numerous as the stars in the sky. Maybe the experts have solutions that will prove beneficial. A lot of things have changed since I was in school. One should be open to all aspects and hope to connect with their learning style.

Perhaps the keyword in all this is *intervention*. The sooner the disability is recognized, the sooner the system can intervene and help the poor, floundering student. Let's not let another one slip through the cracks.

As I got older and more confident. I learned to advocate for myself. I talked to teachers and those that instruct and told them of my disability. Most said, "Have someone type your papers for you." This daunting and terrifying not to mention time-consuming process could be accomplished by simply having someone type my papers. Wow, that old adage "the squeaky wheel gets the most grease" holds true. The more I tried to conceal my disability, the harder I made it on myself.

At first encounter, most people would not realize I have a problem, nor would I expect them to. I've been asked to take charge of some community event or volunteer for a position beyond my capabilities. Hey, I can't even do my own income taxes. I tried three times, and three times I got audited. I find it best to stay away from things I can't do.

My mother was born in 1907. She was half French and half Indian. The Indians call it Mites (mixed blood). She was born on the Belcourt Indian reservation in the Turtle Mountains. Her name was Margret Plante. When she was little, she could speak only French. The government sent her to Fort Totten Indian School. Most of the Indian kids spoke French and Indian. My great-great-great-grandfather on my mom's side came from France. They were fur traders. They married Indian women.

My grandma was born 1868. She died 1948, a year before I was born. She had thirteen kids. My mother was the baby of the family, just as I am the baby of the family. If our family goes back two generations, it is equivalent to four normal generations. I find when I speak to most people, their grandparents are the same age as my parents. I guess I sound like a fibber, but I can relate to what someone says twenty years older than me.

Oh, I forgot to mention, one of my uncles played football with the great Jim Thorpe. He was one of the four horsemen at Carlisle Indian School. His name was Daniel Plante. Daniel was there in 1910 when he was eighteen.

I read somewhere that the government placed all these different Indian tribes at Carlisle. Some were archenemies. A few years earlier, there was a lot of fighting among the students. The shortsighted government officials never took this into consideration and placed them all in one spot. Cowabunga, eh?

Carlisle is in Pennsylvania. It is said over 140 different tribes were assembled there. Throughout the years, ten thousand students went there from its beginning to closing.

vii

I remember going to a lot of Indian pow wows when I was little. Mother and Dad would dress up in Indian gear—ribbons, bells. Dad would put on a headdress. They loved to dance at the pow wow. They had a lot of friends.

Mom had a lot of cousins who dressed up in costumes. On the other hand, my skin was two shades lighter than the rest. For me, it was fighting time. Mom had to watch me. We stopped going to pow wows when I was about ten years old. Family members started dying off, and the parents were getting old. I was on always on the side of the Indian and their plight to get their settlements and to make right the wrong that was done to them. After all, I am quarter Indian. My dad was born in 1901. He was born at Fort Rice, North Dakota. My great-grandmother came from Austria to North Dakota 1882. She was a widow with seven kids. My grandfather was eleven years old at that time. They lived in Fort Rice, about ten miles south of Mandan. It is said that Grandma and the kids would collect buffalo bones in an old ox cart below the cliffs and take them to Mandan and sell them. They came to Mandan for the free land. Everyone got eighty archers. All this is written down by the Morton County Historical Society There were two boys and five girls. My dad got drafted in the First World War. They put him in the cavalry. They figured anyone from North Dakota could ride a horse.

When I was little, we used to own a bar. We called it the Coyote Bar. It was an interesting place for a small kid. We had guns above the bar and around the room. We also had a large moose head hanging in the room. Along the bottom of the bar was a long brass rail. The bar itself was an impressive long mahogany structure that had a cretin ambiance about it. This added to the flavor of the bar. It was a picture out of the old west.

On the floor was a large steel grate. As kids, we would take broom handles and put a piece of gum on the handle of the broom then stick the broom handle through the grate and get the coins that the customers dropped. The grate was the cover for a gravity-fed furnace. This heated the bar. I remember Dad always wore cowboy boots and a cowboy hat. I'd never seen him without his boots and hat. Now Dad was pretty clever. If he wanted the bar swept, he would say to the bums, "Who wants to sweep the bar room floor for a free beer?"

Generally, he would get no response. Then he would throw a few quarters on the floor, then he would shout, "Hey, I found a quarter." A few seconds later, he would say, "I found another quarter!" Pretty soon the bums would be fighting over the broom. I remember they used to call undesirables dehorns. Maybe it was a slang term. The locals referred to the bar as the bloody bucket; it was a pretty rough place. The clientele we construction workers and young people who loved to hoot and holler. Most loved to fight as a form of entertainment. I remember going in the bar in the morning and seeing blood splattered on the walls. Once the front bay window was boarded up. I asked, "What happened?" They said a customer jumped through pane glass window. They said someone was chasing him with a broken beer bottle.

I was taught early a good work ethic. I took my older brother Bob's shoe-shining kit and started shining shoes. I charged 25 cents a shine. Not only did I work my dad's bar, I also did all the bars down the avenue. I remember going from customer to customer, "Hey, mister, do you want a shine?" Once I had a woman who wanted her shoes polished. She had one-fourth-inch strap shoes. I took out my liquid black polish. I tried my best to do them straps, but I kept getting polish on her nylons.

And every time I touched her nylons, the whole bar would burst out laughing. I was a sweaty mess. Eventually someone came up to me and gave me a dollar and told me to get out of there. I kind of think she was moving her foot on purpose. I guess the joke was on me. One had to know their territory. Every neighborhood had their own shoeshine boy. One could get beat up straying too far from home. I guess I had maybe six bars I took care of.

I had a friend named Billy. He was ingenious. I asked him how he got his money. He told me he had the telephone route. I asked him, "What's that?" He swore me to secrecy. I crossed my heart and swore before God not to tell anyone. He said he had all booths up and down the avenue. Back then all the coin slots used to be open. Billy would stick cotton up them slots so the return coins would not return. He said he made pretty good money at it. The telephone route was never mentioned again. Billy and I were friends for life. Bill always had something going on the side, and there always seemed to be a little twist to it.

I was thinking about Ma. She had an interesting life. She told me about her friend Evelyn Frechette. Evelyn was also a Metis. She went to Flandreau Indian School in South Dakota, same as my mom and her sister. She was a friend

x

of the family. Evelyn was also the gangster John Dillinger's girlfriend, the lady in red. Evelyn had a show at the state fair (crime does not pay). She would put on her red dress and answer questions from the customers. After the shows, she would come up to our place and visit with my mother. Mom said she would wear her red dress when she came to visit.

Mom work at the Saint Paul Hotel during roaring twenties. She was a cleaning woman. Mom would go into the speakeasy and party. One time her and a girlfriend went up to a room and partied with a bunch of guys. The next day, her girlfriend showed her the newspaper, and she said, "They just shot your boyfriend." The newspaper said, "Baby Face Nelson Killed." Mom kept a lot of things to herself; she took a lot of things to the grave with her. The roaring twenties have a lot of gray areas. Our family tree needs some answers.

Sister Jean

Sister Jean and Jim were twins they were born in 1948. Jean was tiny and quite athletic. She used to play on the swing set and people would come out of the bar and watch her. She would do a few tricks and people would give her money. I remember when she was little she got her Musketeers ears in the mail. She was an official Mickey Mouse club member, I was Jell-us. Jean growing up was pretty popular always had a lot of friends. As Jean grew up and went to High School she was a Princess a number of years at Machanic Arts. Her senior year she was Homecoming Queen. Jean graduated in 1966 bought a couple of furniture stores and is doing well.

Christopher Platzer

Chris was my youngest son never caused any problems always had a big heart he was a gentle soul. Born in 1974. He is very creative and can do most things. He took the Tri State motor cycle award for creative innovation and was featured in a motor cycle magazine. I was thinking about his early childhood. I remember when he was maybe 1 ½ I had bought a gas operated airplane of modal planes one would fly around in the back yard. I told myself I bought it for the kids. I had trouble starting the plane so I brought it inside and was working it on the kitchen table. I was so focused on the plane I didn't notice Chris had climbed up on a chair and was holding a bottle of fuel in his hands the cap was off. The bottle of fuel had a skull and crossbones on the label in big red letters it said poison. I looked at him and said did you drink any of that stuff? His only vocabulary was yup. I rushed him to the hospital, explained the situation showed them the bottle. They took a blood test and everything was OK no sign of fuel in his bloodstream. They gave me some medication to make him throw up when I got home. I had answer a lot of questions about child abuse and felt like a criminal when I left the hospital. Outside of a few small incidents he was a good kid.

Wrestling champ Ron Brown well know in the wrestling world. He graduated from the school of hard knocks. And managed to survive. Hats off to Ron.

Brother Joe

Brother Joe was born in 1928. He was twenty-one years older than me. He was already out of the house before I was born. Joe went into the service toward the end of the Second World War. He was in the airborne force (paratroopers). He belonged to the Hells Angels. He told me his Hells Angels patch was worth a lot of money. Joe said his job in the service was island hopping. He said they would go to different Islands and tell the Japanese the war was over. He said he went on this one island and they found a large cave with a Japanese mint inside. Joe said there were stacks and stacks of money. He said there was all kinds of equipment, printing press, and whatever it takes to do such things. Joe sent home a bunch of Japanese money. He also had a large Japanese flag and a large Japanese sword. I think he also had a Japanese rifle. I remember when I was young, every now and then we would get some Japanese money.

Brother Ken

Brother Ken was born in 1931. He was in the Korean War. Ken was in the Marines. He said he was a shoemaker. He told me that the North Koreans overran his camp. He said he and another guy were busy making boots; they worked all night, and when they looked outside in the morning, everyone was gone. He said they had to sneak back to their own lines. He said they got some kinda medal for it. I heard my parents talking about Ken. They said Ken was on leave, drinking a beer in uniform at the bar. When a man started to hassle him. They said he turned around and punched the guy. They said it was a one-punch fight. He knocked the guy out with one punch.

I also heard that once the bar was full of soldiers, someone set off some firecrackers. Ma said everyone hit the deck. Not a person was standing in the bar. Could have heard a pin drop.

Brother Jim

Brother Jim was born in 1948. He is a year older than me. Jim was in the Vietnam War. He was drafted into the army in 1966. Jim was a cook in the army hospital. He said most of his activity was centered around the hospital. He said the worst job was he had to talk to those about to die and the wounded who were coming in He said the doctors would walk by and shake their heads, no chance. The dying would ask for the doctors. He would tell them the doctors would be coming along soon.

Thinking about the time when brother Jim got his new old Buick. He got it real cheap. This was a 1954 Buick with a hydro flow transmission. I guess this was one of the many faults of this particular model.

xiv

We decided to go hunting with a few friends that Saturday. We were going to hunt grouse, rabbits, squirrels—anything considered small game. We went to Carlos Avery game reserve, which was about fifteen miles from home. It was a nice, sunny day when we got there. We went out into the woods and went our separate ways. A few hours later it became overcast. This kinda disoriented everything. I came to the conclusion I was lost. Nothing gets the old heart ticking as when you're lost. I stumbled around for half an hour. When I ran into my brother Jim, he said he was glad to see me—'cause he was lost. Wow, no sense telling him I was lost too. I just said, "Follow me." I bluffed my way out of the woods. We ended about a half mile from the car.

We drove a mile down the road and found our friends. They were happy to see us. We were all happy to be heading home. We got about halfway home when all three forward gears went out. The only gear we had left was reverse. By then we were so hungry we ate field com. We had to drive the rest of the way home in reverse. We got home around dark.

Myself Tom

I was born in 1949. I went and enlisted in 1967, the year I graduated. It was a bad year. I went to enlist (my draft number was so high I never would have got called) and took the psychical at the Naval Air station at the Minneapolis airport (passed). For some reason, the swear-in date was

xv

two months away. In the meantime, my dad passed away. A few weeks after that, we got a notice from Social Security saying we owed three months' back pay. I was the only one home at the time. My mother had no source of income. I went down to the draft board and told them of my situation. I told them that I had to stay home and make house payments and pay bills. Plus, I already had a brother in Vietnam. They said they couldn't give me a deferment. They took my application and put it under this huge stack of papers and said, "Have a good life." Was it divine intervention? Was it providence? Who knows? My brother said with my gung-ho attitude, I probably would have been killed right away. He said I was small enough that they probably would have been made a tunnel rat out of me.

There you have it, our family had four wars in one family. My dad was in the First World War, my brother Joe Second World War, my brother Ken the Korean War, and last but not least, Jim in the Vietnam War. I guess our family gave a pretty good contribution to our country

Holidays

When I was young, we would all get together on holidays. There were seven of us siblings. Christmas was special. There were presents stacked so high one could hardly see the tree. I remember Dad waiting to the last minute to buy the tree so he could get the cheapest price. What fun we had decorating the tree. Most of the trees we bought were picked over. They always had bald spots, or they were

xvi

crooked or maybe had a broken spot. We always put the bad spot next to the wall. We would fight over who got to put on the bulbs and tinsel and light bulbs. Everyone got to add their special touch. I don't think Dad ever paid more than two dollars a tree. I guess that was the fun of it. I use to worry maybe we might not have a tree, but he always came through. I remember we always had an angel or star on top of the tree. Yup, we had the best tree.

I remember the family would go to midnight mass so they could sleep in Christmas day. Everyone would come over after church and eat and have a few drinks. I think they let us kids open one present. Then we would all meet together Christmas day.

Thanksgiving was another big family get-together. We always had a large turkey and all the fixings—mashed potatoes, gravy, hot buns, cranberry sauce, salads. Everybody brought something. As the old Chinese proverb "Many hands make small work," so we had cakes, pumpkin pies, cookies, fruit salads, and plenty of strong drinks. Everyone brought a bottle. Joe, Bobby Jim, my dad—all were bartenders. Me, Jim, and Jean were the small kids. We always got the dark meat—a drumstick or a wing. The white meat was saved for the adults.

There's something about a large family. There's a feeling of security; it's like they're always going to be there. It's like an umbrella always there to protect you. Those were the days. Mother once told me, "Only your family loves your antics. Outsiders might not like it. So be aware and be selective." Every now and then I forget that rule.

Dad

Dad was great as far as fathers go. He always spent time with us kids. He would always take us fishing. I was kind of a ritual. We would always find an old tin can then head for Uncle Toni's. There we would go in his garden and dig angle worms. Tony had a beautiful place. He had a big yard with maybe ten apple trees and a rhubarb patch that was kid friendly. We used to pick a bunch of rhubarb and bring it home and make rhubarb sauce.

Tony also had a large currant patch. We used to pick a couple of grocery bags of currant and make jams and jellies. He also had raspberry and strawberries. He also had a large pond in the back. Us kids would spend hours catching frogs and tadpoles, every once in a while a salamander. We went home many times with wet shoes and pants. It was always a fun-filled day at Uncle Tony's, but mostly we went fishing. Our favorite spot was Sucker Creek. We would spend hours fishing. We used cane poles. We used to tie them to the top of the car. A guy can get pretty handy with a cane pole. Sucker Creek had a hand pump well. This well had the coldest and best-tasting well water around.

On our fishing excursions, we usually used all the angle worms up. That was a signal it was time to go home. We had a little setup at home, a little table and two little chairs. Dad taught us how to clean fish a few times, then we were on our own. I had to do the scaling, Jim the cutting. Jim cut because Dad thought I was too small to handle a knife. We always wrapped the fish heads and guts in newspaper. It seemed to me the garbage can was always full of maggots.

They seemed to be entertaining in themselves, all of them little larvae crawling around. Cool.

Sometimes our little friends would come over when we were cleaning fish. They would end up throwing up. Jim and I figured they were kinda delicate. After the fish were cleaned, we would take them up to Ma. She would fry them up. She would salt and pepper them, then dust them in flour, then fry them nice and crispy. There is a certain art to eating sunfish. There's a certain protocol one must follow. If you're not careful, you will get a mouth full of bones. I'm not going to divulge this information. I might have been sworn to secrecy. But if done right, one can eat a plateful of sunnies as fast as you can fry them. Dad always had a plate of bread at the table in case one happened to choke on a bone. One could not be too safe when eating fish. Our summers were not filled with just fishing. In the fall of the year, we used to catch frogs when the frogs were running. We had our gunnysacks and flashlights, and we would catch frogs for eating. They were easy to clean. We used to throw the frog legs in a pie pan and soak them. Then we put salt on them and watched them jump. They would also jump when one would start frying them.

Now Dad had an uncanny ability to spot wild fruit. He would be driving along and would spot some choke-cherries, stop, and say, "Go pick them chokecherries." We would take them home and make chokecherry jelly. He did that with hazelnuts. We would pick a sack of them, then bring them home and dry them out. Later we'd eat them. He knew where the raspberries and strawberries were, all this stuff, and when they were in season.

Our dad had a cultural side. Once or twice a month, we would go the science museum or maybe the history museum. I myself preferred the science museum. There they had the mummies and dinosaurs. I could spend hours looking at that stuff. Sometimes we would go to both museums. And every once in a while, we would go to the state capital. We would walk around and be amazed at how big everything was. I guess you could say we were well rounded.

The fifties were a transitional period. The carefree environment of preschool children was now gone. Life started pretty normal, it seemed to me, except for bloody noses and migraine headaches. I've had them since I can remember. I didn't think anything was abnormal. I used to get bad nosebleeds. I would sit over the toilet and watch the large drops of blood make large rings in the water. I would sit there for a long time till my nose stopped bleeding. If I tilted my head back, I would choke on my own blood. This bloodletting had a positive side; it would relieve the pressure in my head, and my migraine headaches would go away. I remember back then it didn't take much to get a bloody nose. It is said I was born with my umbilical cord wrapped around my neck. Was it lack of oxygen that caused my disability? Who knows? No more hiding behind Ma's apron. The harsh realities of an unkind world was starting to reveal itself. Street cars were leaving the scene. Baby boomers were everywhere. I was excited.

My brother and sister were a year older than me. When they started school, I would miss them. Now I had no one to play with. I couldn't wait for school to start for me so I could make new friends.

Summer was kind as always. Swimming, playing, interacting with other kids—life was great. I couldn't wait for school to start so I could make new friends, play and share, laugh and do things that children do.

Back in the fifties, school was a little different. Teachers could hit you. A child was taught respect for their elders and how adults were always right. After the first few weeks of school, my vision of school was quickly crushed. I didn't know I was different from other kids. It seems I was a problem for the teachers. They didn't know what to do with learning-disabled child. They used to believe they could beat competence into the child. They beat me. I was hit and punched, and with all this attention, I was still not conforming. Worse yet, I could not tell my right hand from my left. I think I should have been left-handed (I have a son who is left-handed). I went to a Catholic school. They said the world had no need for left-handed people. They would hit me every time I used my left hand. We used to have morning inspections. Everyone stood in line and had to hold out their hands. They would inspect for dirty hands and dirt under the fingernails. If any dirt was found, they would hit you across the fingers with one of them oak blackboard pointers. You were also hit if your shirt was not tucked in. Now when they hit you, they made sure your palm was pointing down. This way they could hit you across the knuckles. Now a seven-year-old's hands are not very big, and even a light tap would seem to hurt.

We used to live four blocks from school. There were many obstacles along the way to school. Our path to school led us through Lawson playgrounds. My inquisitive nature seem to entrap me. I had a hands-on nature. I seemed to have to touch everything. I found I hated wearing gloves. I felt that I could not feel the texture of things. My little boy ways were setting me up for morning inspection. There was another fly in the ointment; they would want to see our hankies. If you didn't use your hanky right, you got hit. Hanky protocol called for you to use all four corners of the hanky before using the center. If found using the center first, you got hit. Hey, I was a seven-year-old with a sinus condition. It was just another trap for me.

Some nuns were just plain mean. Once at playtime, we were instructed to build the tallest building we could with our play blocks. I built the tallest. I was kinda proud. A nun came over and kicked my building over, saying I built it wrong. She offered no advice, and her voice rang with disdain. St. Benard's was a German church with a German congregation. I guess their stern discipline was an offshoot of an antiquated practice. I talked to other people who went Catholic schools. They talked about how stern their discipline was. I believe my school was one of the worst.

Life experiences help mold our personality. I remember thinking, *One day I will grow out of this*. Well, you never really do. You learn to work with it. You have to work outside the box. I could not meet standard performance, but I excelled in other areas; I was good in art. I was good in sports.

Come to think of it, that's the only thing I was good at. I learned to conceal my handicap. A lot of things in life could not be achieved. I could not preform. I could not meet expectations. Many jobs require certain skills, such as typing reports, spelling, and a lot of written communication

They were going to hold me back in third grade because I couldn't read. That summer, my mother bought me a large box of comic books. I paged through them. My mother said if I read the words, the books will mean more. I knew how to make the vowel sounds. It was painstakingly slow, but I learned to pronounce the words. The more I read, the better I got. By the end of summer, I could read. Yippee I couldn't wait to go back to school and show everyone. Of course, this was a slow process. It was increments, but little by little, progress was made.

A little peek into my mind, when I spell a word, there's no picture in my mind, it's blank, so I have to sound the word out and spell it phonetically. A lot of the classes I took even in college, I could not spell. *Physics* starts with an *F* for me. It took two years for me to spell my high school's name, Mechanic Arts High School. That silent *h* got me every time.

My dad owned a bar. I remember doing pushups for money at a very early age, maybe seven years old. Ten pushups for a dime. These pushups were making me strong. I had uncanny strength for my age. I seemed to be building a reputation as a tough guy. I learned quickly if anyone made fun of my disability, I could beat them up. This was my protection; no one dared make fun of me.

I remember misspelling a word. The teacher made me write the word a hundred times on the blackboard. The next day, I misspelled the word again (third or fourth grade).

I seemed to hang with a tough crowd. I really didn't notice. We all respected each other. I was surprised thirty years later to find out that one of my best friends was dyslexic. I didn't find out till I went to night school for the learning disabled.

The day I left the Catholic school, I had a nun beat me up one day. She punched me and shook me so hard she tore my shirt off. I was so scared. The next day, I hid under the bed. My brother and sister were twins. They were a year older. When they came home from school, I climbed out from under the bed and went right behind them. We all yelled, "We're home!"

My mother said, "Jim and Jean are home, early teachers' meeting. You should have two hours of school left."

I told her what happened the day before. I showed her my torn shirt with all the buttons torn off. She saw the bruises on my chest and was outraged. She told me I was going back to school with her. When we got to school, she made me wait outside. As I waited, I could hear her yelling throughout the school, a mama bear defending her cub. When she came out, she said I would not have to go back to that school. I heard many years later that they took that nun out of that school after many complaints.

Fourth grade, Ms. Fogerty one of the biggest influences in my life. She was gentle and kind. She taught poetry. I learned rhyme and meter. I learned ten poems in her class I can still recite today. Ms. Fogerty used to fall asleep reciting her poetry. Some say she was bitten by a tsetse fly, some kinda African insect, yet her love of poetry gave me an outlet and a small hold on the written language.

Ms. Darch she was an egotist. She wore way too much makeup. She was almost scary to look at. She would brag how the high school would compliment her on how well her students were taught and how each one was a feather in her cap. She would make a knuckle with her middle finger and rap you on the head for punishment. I believe she had a sore knuckle by the time I got out of her class.

The grade school I went to must have had a contract with the Dairy Queen because they gave a free ice cream cone with every A on the report card. There were long lines at the Dairy Queen. I never had to wait. I never got an A. As far as grades go, a C was like an A to me. Most of my report cards were generally bad. Most of my report cards said, "He can do better." This phrase seemed to resonate throughout my schooling.

I remember most of the kids I hung around with seemed to have similar problems. We were all underachievers. Most of my friends seemed to get into trouble. Most were on probation. I had an abundance of common sense. I seemed to know when it was time to leave before they got in to trouble.

I remember Billy and I decided to raise pigeons. We would go under bridges and crawl along the I beams and check the nest for baby birds. This was dangerous work; we could fall to the tracks below. One could choke on the smoke from the trains. We probably got six pigeons before the novelty wore off. We used to check the empty box cars for grain and corn so we could feed the baby pigeons. Later we would ride the empty box cars just for fun.

We used to walk around the neighborhood, walking around the curbs, looking for cigarette butts. We picked up the best ones and smoked them. We did have a standard; they had to be so long and not too much lipstick on them. We thought we were cool. Yup, those were the days. Funny we didn't get some kinda disease. Some of us did it for amusement. Others became addicted.

I remember I couldn't wait to graduate and start working. I had a brother working at Swift & Company. He pulled some strings and go me a job. I started about a week after school was out. I started in the canned ham department. We would cut hams and put them in cans. The cans would come down a conveyor belt. I was to fill every third can. We mostly did five-pound hams. Each station had its own scale. We had to cut the ham to size, throw it in the can, then it would proceed to a machine that put the lid on the cans. Then the cans were put in a large metal basket, maybe two hundred hams, then sent to the cooker. The cooker had large tanks of water he would put the baskets in the water, and it would cook the hams, maybe for four hours, then they were boxed and sent to the customer.

All the cutters had to wear a white robes and metal hats and rubber boots. We all had knife trays with four knifes, a sharpening stone, a hone, and one meat hook. We would spend the last half hour of our day sharpening our knives for the next day. On the line one had to be fast. If you could not keep pace, you were quickly replaced and sent somewhere else in the planet. We had to run the equipment at a certain rate. The company had a quota; anything above the quota was bonus money. We knew just how much to put out so we would get twenty dollars extra a week. If we went too much over our quota, they would raise the quota.

The packing houses were all in the same place Swift, Armers, Hormel. They all used the same stockyards. The stockyards were large corrals where they kept the livestock for slaughter

When I started working for Swift, the employees were getting up in age. I guess one could say they were getting close to retirement. The place was starting to deteriorate. Everything had an old look to it. I guess you could say it was scheduled for teardown.

I learned a valuable lesson, or you could say experience. I was young and strong. I was sent to load box cars with boxes of canned hams. The boxes weighed forty pounds apiece. We started out with three guys. They were older guys. By the end of the day, I was the only one working. I asked where everyone was. Someone said if I was going to do the work of three men, they would let me. They were in the locker room smoking and playing cards. It taught me never go into a situation and apply your work ethic. Let them set the pace. I had a strong work ethic taught at an early age. There have been a few times I regretted it. I guess I was overeager in most cases.

The poor attitude was like a cancer; it prevailed throughout the plant. You could go in any locker room, and there would be a pall of smoke hanging in the air. The benches would be full of workers not on their jobs. The workers had created their own demise. The plant shut down two and half years after I started. The group I worked with were hard workers, but this was not the case all over. The brown and serve department was all women. They worked very hard. They did sausages and hot dogs. They were after the bonus money.

I remember growing up, our mother would tell us stories. They were lesson stories. Most were morality based. We were taught to respect elders and be kind to cripple people or anyone with an abnormality that made them different. This was probably the Indian side. I guess it's traditional to pass on history through stories.

Honesty was a big thing in our house. If money was on the kitchen table, we were not to touch it. Mother said whoever owns that money will be back for it, "It's not yours. It is not for the taking." I remember friends would come over. They would say, "Take the money."

I would tell them, "It is not mine. It is not for me to take. The owner will be back for it."

My little friends were a band of thieves. They would take anything not nailed down. They would even take money out of their own mother's purse.

I guess my house became the topic of discussion. Some came to see this phenomena, where money would stay on the table. I remember what mother used to say about crippled people, "Just be thankful it isn't you." These were things I learned to respect, and I admonished my friends when they felt the need to make fun someone.

I remember we were taught as kids how to cook. We were taught how to make breakfast. Each of us would take a turn once a week. There were three of us. We learned to fry eggs, pancakes, waffles, sausage, fried potatoes, toast—

every aspect of breakfast. My mother thought these would be skills that we would need later on in life.

As we got older, we were taught how to make supper. We were taught how to make roasts, chicken, turkey, gravy, hamburgers, fried fish, just about anything. Even today I use the skill Mother taught me. I never got into making cakes and pies. I remember Mother used to make bread and doughnuts. Never did that ether. When Mother would make supper, she always put a couple of extra potatoes in the oven just in case company would come over. Company was always welcome at our house. If nothing else, we would fry the extra potatoes up for breakfast. I was the biggest recipient of Mother's stories. Maybe because I was the baby. When I brought up the stories to my brother and sister, they said they never heard of such things. It was news to them.

Later on in life, I was surprised to find out that people can't cook. Hot dogs and TV dinners are the extent of their cooking knowledge. When I was a kid, I went to a friend's house for dinner. His mother gave us each a plate of elbow noodles. I waited for something else, nothing, no bread, no sauce, no meatballs, only butter. He put butter on his noodles, and this was his meal. He didn't see anything wrong with this.

At my house, we would have maybe roast beef, mashed potatoes, gravy, green beans, and some kind of fruit. A friend mine said he thought we were rich by the way we made big meals. This was our way of life. We didn't know what hunger was. Back in the day, supper was served hot and ready. When Dad came home from work, all of us had to wash our hands and be waiting when Dad sat down. Then we would bow our heads and say grace. I guess it was a different world back then.

Every summer, we would go on vacation. It is said my mother was a little gypsy because she loved to travel and see different things. We would go to the badlands or Yellow Stone Park, maybe Mount Rushmore, and many other places. We stayed in tents or slept in the car. We would stop at a grocery store and buy lunch, meat and bread, and make lunch on the fly.

I remember getting home sick after a day on the road. I remember I missed my friends. Mom would buy me a little bottle of Mogen David wine. This would help me keep quiet, and I would fall asleep.

Back in those days, we didn't have air conditioning in the car. We had all the windows rolled down. There would be hands and feet sticking out of all the windows

Papers

I remember in grade school when I had to write a little paper in class, and I would get the paper back. There would be red ink all over the paper. The teacher would have to write three times the amount that I would, correcting my errors. I hope she didn't get writer's cramp. I guess she needed to show what an expert she was in English. Or maybe she bought the red pens on sale. All I know is, she didn't have the vision to see that there was something wrong. Or she was not aware there was such a thing as a learning disability. Or maybe she thought all her suggestions would help me. Bless her heart for investing all that time in me. I bet with all her effort, she could make a blind man see. I had many teachers correct my papers. And I proved to be a challenge. Most teachers were generous and gave me a grade above an F. I didn't care what grade I got just so I passed. I remember throwing away my report cards so no one would see them.

Franklin Language Master 4000 with Pronouncing Dictionary and Thesaurus—wow, this little handheld spell checker saved my butt many times. I found it invaluable. If I misspelled a word, it would give me a large selection of words to choose from. I would pick out a word and hit the say button, and it would pronounce the word for me. Then there is the thesaurus that gives you the explanation of the word. I found some of the words I selected were not proper for my papers and would not work as intended. I used this machine on all my papers. My papers were time consuming. They would take hours and hours to complete. A simple paragraph would have to be written out in longhand. Then I would have to correct everything. Then I would type the paper using the one-finger pecking process, then proofread and find out that I omitted a few keywords then retype the papers again.

We moved around a lot. We moved to Frogtown when I was eleven. I made a new set of friends. We had a great neighborhood, a lot of little friends. We played hide-and-seek. It was an age where boys and girls still played together. I had a little girlfriend who would do my homework so I would have more time to play. She was so sweet, but I was too shy or stupid to do anything about it. It was puppy love for me. And I was brokenhearted when she moved away.

The following year, the boys and the girls separated. The boys hung out together, and the girls went their separate ways. The boys would play sports, baseball, football, street hockey sometimes into the night under the streetlight. My family owned a grocery store, and we all hung around my place. It was kind the neighborhood gathering place. We had a ma-and-pa grocery store. I believe my brother and I ate all the little store's profits. We just hung around, being cool.

I remember we all had bikes and the carefree days of just riding around. That's when I got my first new bike, my twelfth birthday. We went down to Montgomery Wards, and I got to pick my own bike out. It was a red one. I remember we put cards on the spokes so it sounded like a real motor. Well, time passed, and the summer was over. It was time to go back to school. I went to Mechanics Arts High School. This was a mixed race school. We had blacks, Mexicans, Indians whites. Everyone seemed to get along. We lived about a mile from school.

The first day of school, I did not know what to expect. When I was about two blocks from school, I saw a gang of blacks on one side of the street, then there was a gang of Mexicans on the other side of the street. They were shouting at each other. I didn't know what to do. I waited for the traffic light to turn green and walked down the center stripe past the gangs.

The first day was a half day. We spent most of it getting our class schedules. Since everyone was new, it took a while to get acquainted. No one knew about my disability. The teachers treated everyone the same.

I remember the first day of gym class. We had wrestling class. There was a big black gym leader. He pointed at me and said, "I'll wrestle that chubby white kid." I pinned him in about a minute. The whole gym class got quiet. I just beat one of the best athletes in school. I guess the word got around. I never had a problem with any of the students after that day.

As the days began to settle down, my disability began to manifest itself. I found myself in a couple of remedial classes. Wow, I was top of the class. I could answer all the questions. I could read all the material. So this is how it is to be top of the class. Well, this lasted about two weeks. The teacher said I didn't belong in this class. He sent me back to regular class. Oh well, here I am again back to the bottom, the poorest-performing student in class. The only thing I was good at was art and gym. I got As in art and gym. I was good at golf, football, swimming, wrestling. I lettered in all them sports. I excelled in football, made the all-city team. I made All State player of the week twice. I even won a scholarship in football. I gave it away. I had no intention of continuing school. I made art student of the year my senior year. They would announce my achievements over the loudspeakers, but I never heard them. When I'm concentrating, I block everything out. The last day of school, the principal told me he had some more awards in his office for me. I went to his office. He never showed up.

Counterfeiting

That is one of them things one never gives much thought to. A friend of mine got a job working at Ramsey Hospital He worked in the mimeograph department after school. I stopped up and visited him, and he showed me all the equipment he had to run. He had to make notepads and pamphlets for staff meetings. He said he also had a photocopier, and it would copy anything, so I pulled a dollar bill out of my wallet, and said, "Will it copy this?" (No problem.) The copy came out black and white, and it only copied one side, but still it looked okay. Now we had to copy both sides and staple them together.

"Well, this is kinda cool. Let's make about fifty of them so we can play poker with them."

So we did, fifty backs and fronts and stapled them together. It was kinda cool. They looked good in the dark. A couple of weeks went by, and I kinda forgot about them. I gave a few to my dad. He thought they were cool. He played a few tricks on the bartender, had some laughs. Well, a couple of these fake dollars fell into the wrong hands. There was a blind vendor working at Capitol building. Two kids tried to buy cigarettes from the vender. The vender called the cops right away. The students were arrested, and they called the FBI, so the students told the FBI where they got the money.

The next day, they called the whole school through the principal's office. Of course they made me and John be the last ones to be questioned. They told me and John that we were counterfeiting, and if we did this again, we would get

xxxiv

twenty years in prison The FBI agents had on black trench coats and black hats. They were the real deal. They put handcuffs on me and put me in a black car in the back seat with no handles, not even for the widows. They drove me home to my parents. They told them if I got caught counterfeiting again, I would get twenty years. I gave them what money I had left. My dad scolded me in front of them. I have not counterfeited again.

Two weeks out of school, I started a job at Swift & Company.

In 1968, I met my wife. We got married in 1969. I was too young to get married. My mother had to sign for me. One had to be twenty-one; I was only twenty. Well, the marriage lasted twelve years, and I got two good boys out of the deal. They never caused me any problems, and I'm proud of both of them.

I worked at the same place forty-two and a half years. We changed hands five times. The last owner was Curwood. Curwood said at our introduction meeting that they could not meet our quality or productivity, so they bought us. Took our technology, eliminated there competition. They shut us down in two years. I guess that's the way it goes.

When I was young, my dad owned a bar. When he had someone fix something, he had me go watch them. If he had a hot water heater replaced, he would say, "Watch them so you know how next time." Same thing with Sheetrock, carpentry, plumbing—anything the required some degree of skill.

There were many skills I learned and could use in my walk through life. The first house I bought was a duplex. I

xxxv

knew how to make repairs from what I learned as a child. There was hardly anything I couldn't do. I had boundless energy. I guess you could say that I was a jack-of-all-trades and a master of none. I applied what I leaned on the buildings I owned throughout my life. Then I bought forty acres of land and built a house. I called it my hunting shack. It was a two-bedroom rambler with running water, shower, toilet, laundry room, and fireplace. Thought it might be my retirement home. Later I built a five-car garage, seventy-two feet long. I put five garage doors on it. All this I built on overtime money. Later I would buy another forty adjoining acres. Now I had eighty acres to play in. I had a mile of walking trails put in, built a rock wall, and had a field cut out so I could watch the deer play. I planted fruit trees, apple and pear trees, and put in a big fire pit for bonfires.

I meet Phyllis on the Internet just about the same time I got done building the place. Somehow I lost her in the cloud. Didn't know how to use the computer to well. A month later, she gets ahold of me and ask what happened. I told her I somehow deleted her and didn't know how to find her. We talked on the phone. She seemed to like everything I did. I told her I worked a lot of overtime. She seemed to be okay with that. She lived in Cloquet, twenty miles north of Moose Lake, Minnesota. I was helping a friend move close to that area and told I would meet her at Moose Lake for dinner. We had dinner and talked. She liked everything I did. We both liked antiques. We both were homebodies. Our kids were grown. I told her I had to go up to the cabin to tie some rebar for the patio before they poured the cement. She said she knew how to tie rebar.

I said, "Cool, well, come on up."

She came up and stayed the weekend. Her daughter was a little upset that she would go way up north to a cabin with a Wisconsin ax murder.

Phyllis's birthday came. I asked what she would like. She said, "A chain saw."

Cool, now we could clear the fence line together. She's the one for me. Phyllis worked two jobs. One was working for State Farm Insurance. The other was a convenience store job to make ends meet. Somehow she still found the time to come up to the cabin.

Phyllis had a friend who worked for the Saint Paul Insurance Co. She told Phyllis to come down and apply for a job. Phyllis did and got the job. At that time, I owned and lived in a fourplex. Phyllis moved in with me. It was an easy commute to work; the bus was just a block away. In 2005, I sold the fourplex. We bought a place in River Falls. We used to go up to the cabin all the time just to escape the inner city. The serene tranquility of the woods allowed us to recharge and fortify ourselves for another week of city living. Now we live in a neighborhood of big lots. Everyone has an acre and a half. It's peaceful here, no need to get away. We used to have Phyllis's kids come up to the cabin. We would build big bonfires and roast marshmallows poised over the fire with long sticks. We would drink a few cooled beers or some hot chocolate. We always had a large stack of wood for the bonfire. We use to watch the sparks float up in the sky. It was mesmerizing to sit back in your lawn chair and watch for shooting stars. I guess you could call it the good old days.

Divorce was pretty tough on me. I stayed at my sister Jean's house for a year. Bless her heart. In this time, I did a lot of soul-searching. I read the Bible a couple of times. One gathers insight. One gets to know man's nature. It can offer comfort in time of need. I recommend it for those that seek wisdom and piece. I kinda like Ecclesiastes, "All is vanity chasing after the wind." Don't hold anything too precious; it can all be taken away from you. All the effort has been for nothing.

I tried different religions at this time in my life. It seems most offered no solace, kind of a cookie-cutter mentality, a lot of hocus-pocus, a scare tactic that makes you fear for your soul. I kind of think everyone should do a little searching of their own and come up with their own conclusion.

I thought I would write about my struggles going through life with a learning disability, but this book is mostly about poetry that I composed in my mid-thirties and forties. This poetry I needed a lot of assistance with. I could not write or spell a lot of my poetry, I could not read a lot because my spelling was so bad. What I wrote down, it was to conserve the ideas then later figure what I wrote. I would like to thank all the people who assisted me by typing my papers to a legible format so I could share my creation.

A lot of this one-finger typing, or should I say all my typing, requires I look at the keyboard. I spend a lot of my time correcting missing words, or sometimes I will type the whole sentence in capital letters. I took two typing classes. As soon as they covered the keyboards, I was done. Can't remember where the keys are.

A lot of my disability involves names. It used to be I had to work with new people a number of years before I could remember their name. I could read a book, repeat it word for word but not remember the book title or author's name. The teacher would ask, "What books did you read over the summer?" I might have read two or three books but couldn't tell her.

I belonged to a learning disability support group. Had a friend who I knew for five years. I said, "I'm sorry, but I can't remember your name."

He said, "That's okay, I can't remember yours ether."

How cool it is to in an environment where people understand you. That old saying, "Birds of a feather flock together" or the phrase "There is safety in numbers." The compassion and understanding you can receive from people with the same likeness is irreplaceable.

Thank you for all the support. Thank you Learning Disabilities of Minnesota. That provided some schooling that proved invaluable.

I remember when I first started working at American Can. People were rude, and everything they said was condescending. I had a hard time with this. Most were fighting words. I had to restrain myself. They seem to talk that way to everyone. It was as if everyone was trying to outdo each other at being rude. I didn't think I could work in this environment. I started practicing quick replies It was slow, but I evolved. It was against my nature. I practiced rudeness. I

xxxix

started to get good at it, but it was not the real me. I was trapped by vocabulary.

When I was little, I could not express what I wanted to say. This was frustrating. As I evolved, it afforded me some kind of freedom.

I believe this frustration and the search for a way out probably was the foundation for my poetry. As a young kid, I found poetry was thought in rhyme. And for me, it was a way to remember. I remember the lyrics to a couple of hundred songs, but I can't remember song title or the singer. I found I have good face recondition, but I can't attach a name to it. This is so with actors. I can generally remember what show they were in but not their name.

I never learned to punctuate, couldn't tell a noun from a verb or a complete sentence or when to start a paragraph or when to end one. Everything is done by sound. If it sounds right, then it's okay. If you look at my poetry. Most of it is done in capital letters. If there is an upper-and-lower-case combination, then it is typed by someone trying to help me.

I used to have a problem mixing my printing with cursive writing. I would have mixed writing, even mixed words. Half would be print and half cursive.

I went to vocational school three times, one for vending machine repair and twice for prosthetics—once to be a prosthetic technician, the other to be a prosthetic practitioner. Also, I had to complete my two-year degree to get into the practitioner program. Later, I would need my four-year degree for my practitioner program I was one class short of my BA when I decided I didn't deserve it.

I took up prosthetics because I was a good wood carver. Hey, I can carve wooden legs. Well, most legs are plastic and metal. Wood is kind of a lost art. I did learn to make arms and legs. Actually I was pretty good at it. The school's testing method was progressive; as one learned the discipline, one could test out of it. I completed the course, took the national board test, and passed. I was the only one from Minnesota to take the test. The rest were from out of state. I was now a certified prosthetic technician, got my shingle. I knew I would need help with my disability, maybe a lot of tutoring when I went to the collage. I explained my situation to the collage counselors. They said I would need a documented disability, so I went to the University of Minnesota Psychological Department. They tested me and said I had a college level reading ability and a second-grade spelling ability. I thinking I have a retrieval problem. Yup, I'm qualified for tutoring.

The teachers at the college were very understanding. The English teacher in creative writing said I was very creative. The regular English teacher said I could have someone type my papers. Algebra was one of my hardest classes. I devoted many hours to my homework. I would lose sequences A, B, C, terms used to solve equations. I don't believe I ever completed a homework assignment. This is one of the classes I had a tutor in, but I still could not keep up with the class. The teacher knew of my struggle. When it come to the finals, he posted who passed his class. Half the class failed. I passed, yippee! I went to the teacher and talked to him. He asked me if I was ever going to use algebra. I said, "I don't think so." He told me that his son had dyslexia, and he knows how hard it is for me.

I was good at public speaking, and I still got As in art. I finally got my diploma. I now had an AS degree.

When I went back to vocational school and signed up for practitioner school. I did pretty well in the class, but I needed a BA for qualification for the national practitioner test. That was eight hours practical, eight hours written. I came one class short of getting my BA. I didn't want the degree. I didn't want to make a mockery of all those who worked so hard for their degree. I did not want to pursue that profession. I did not trust my ability to retrieve the needed information to do the job.

I remember working for American Can. I operated a machine. I would have to leave a note from time to time. I could not spell half the words I needed in the note. It was unfair to the other shift if there were problem areas that needed addressing before starting the equipment. Lots of time, I would have to stay over till someone showed up so I could verbally convey my message. I did this many times.

High technology improvements made things more difficult. The more things I had to remember, the more things I would forget. After a few costly mistakes, I was asked to step down, so I changed jobs and did things that were less demanding. I went into adhesive blending. This is where I made fifty-gallon drums of glue for big machines called laminates.

Wood carving, I started wood carving in sixth grade in wood shop. We had a choice. We could do a small wood project such as a birdhouse or a bookshelf or maybe do some drafting. The last choice was wood carving. I chose wood carving. Four of us chose wood carving. Wood carving is kinda dangerous. As the other students started to cut themselves, they would drop out. By the end of the course, I was the last one left. I carved a Sottish terrier, looked pretty good. It took first place in a contest. Hey, I'm thinking this wood carving stuff must be my thing.

When I was in high school, my senior art project was a relief carving of a Roman soldier. It came out pretty well. The art teacher give me the wood carving set of tools as a present. Yippee.

Wood carving became a hobby of mine. My preference became relief carving. I learned what kind of wood to carve, how to cut with the grain, the cause and effects of cutting, how to sharpen the cutting tools.

I was carving a civil war scene, signed up for wood-carving class. I brought my project to class. The instructor told me he couldn't help me. He said I knew more than he did. He let me carve with the class, hoping I would be an inspiration to the rest of the class.

I tried different mediums. I worked with clay, metal, fiberglass, wax. I worked at a place where we had twenty-pound chunks of wax. We used to melt it down and put it on paper. It would act as a moisture barrier. As I sat there watching the machine, I would carve little figurines out of the wax, then give them away. I ran into a guy I hadn't seen in twenty years. He said he still had some figurines in his hutch. I carved a figurine of a cowboy and brought it home from work. The wife had some friends over. The husband

xliii

of the wife's friend looked at my statue and said, "Let me make a bronze copy for you."

I said, "Cool, I would love that."

A couple months later, they came over with the bronze statue. This the only thing left of that time period. I wish everything was that easy.

Some experiments were dangerous. I made a plaster bust of a women out of clay, then made a plaster mold out of the clay, then lined the mold with fiberglass resin. It seemed to take forever to dry. My place smelled like fiberglass for weeks.

I had a fifty-gallon fish tank and put the bust in the tank. I thought later I would make a tail simulating a mermaid tail for the other end of the aquarium. About a month later, the fish started getting sores. Here I gave the fish cancer from the fiberglass. Like they say, a little bit knowledge is a dangerous thing. I had a goldfish that was lying on the carpet outside the fish tank. He looked almost dead. One side was dry. I put him back in the tank, and he started to swim. Well, this fish died on one side; the other side kept growing. This fish grew into a circle. And he swam around in circles. It was kinda weird.

I thought I would write this down before I forget. When I first got married around 1970, me and the wife were broke. We were looking around for something to do. I had two dollars to my name. There used to be a produce store on Seventh Street and Payne. They had a sign in front of the store that said, "40 pounds of bananas for a dollar." So I went inside and said, "Give me eighty pounds of bananas."

So I had two big boxes of bananas Told the wife were going to Como Park and feed the monkeys. We got to the park, and I took a shopping bag full of bananas and started throwing bananas to the monkeys. A zookeeper came by. I told him I had 80 pounds of bananas for the monkeys.

He said, "Great, I'll get a dolly. Let's go get them."

So we went around feeding the monkeys inside the safety railings. We actually handed the bananas to the monkeys. Not only did we feed the monkeys outside, he took us downstairs where there were a bunch more monkeys. He said they rotate the monkeys so they get a little privacy. He thanked us for the bananas, and he said it really helps with their budget. He said he wished a lot more people would do such things. He gave us a little plastic gorilla thanked us again, and off we went. I can't help but think that was the best two dollars I ever spent.

When I went to Metro State University, they had a poetry session once a week. I used to read my poetry there. Everyone seemed to like it. There were teachers and students. They would applaud. They even printed one in the school paper. I had one English teacher that came to the poetry session. I had him for a class. He said to me, "Somehow I expected more out of you."

I gave him the best I had. I don't think he realized the wickets I went through just to preform mediocre. I had a few poems printed in some of the vanity books. These are books that print your poetry regardless how good they are, hoping you buy their book at an outrageous price. And your vanity will make you buy it.

I took a course on public broadcasting at Metro State. I took the course at the public broadcasting studio. The condition was I had to produce a segment that was to be televised for public viewing. I did a program on learning disabilities. We used the studio. We had three cameras. I had a psychiatrist and two disability teachers. The program lasted over an hour and showed on public TV for over three months.

I remember when I was young I would write very simple things. I could not write creatively. I could not spell my vocabulary. I wanted to say more, but I had to hold back. It's frustrating to know the answer but not be able to spell it.

Just a note, *psychiatrist* is a word that I spelled so bad that the spell checker on the computer could not find it. Also, my Franklin spell checker could not find it. I had to wait till my wife got home to spell it.

Note, I did run three marathons, the Twin City twice and Grandma's once. The best time I had was 3:38 at Grandma's. The worst was 4:04. One day at prosthetic school, the instructor was watching the New York Marathon on TV. I asked him if he was a runner, and he said no. He said he was looking at prospective customers.

A Few Hunting Stories

I went deer hunting with about eight guys. They were hard-drinking, cigar-smoking, foulmouthed degenerates. I might be exaggerating a little. We were up north to hunt deer. We took the cap off the whiskey bottle and threw it away. We had a lot of whiskey with beer chasers. I was one of the younger ones, didn't know how to pace myself. Maybe I thought I had to prove myself. Anyway I drank more than I should have. We drank till two in the morning, and we had to get up at 5:00 a.m. When it was time to get up, I couldn't do it. I had the worst hangover ever. Thought I was going to die. I told the boys, "You got to go on without me. I am too sick to go hunting." They called me a sissy and a few other things, and then they left without me.

I woke up about 10:00 a.m. feeling much better. I put on my hunting clothes, got my gun, and headed out for the woods. I got about a half a block from the cabin when I saw a deer just standing there, so I shot it; it was a big doe. I gutted her out and dragged her back to the cabin. I hung her in the boathouse to keep the dogs from nibbling on her. Then I went back to bed. The guys came home around noon. They were skunked. They didn't see anything. They'd seen me in bed and called me lazy and a bunch of other names. And shame on me for staying in bed for so long. I said I got my deer.

"Well, where is it?"

I told them to look in the boathouse. They couldn't believe their eyes. Everyone was impressed. I heard nothing but praise after that.

I was up at the cabin deer hunting with a couple of friends. The first day was kinda slow, so we headed to the bar to see how the deer reports were going. My neighbor was sitting at the bar talking to someone. He said he was going to drive his property the next morning. Drive means to form a line of hunters and walk a certain area to chase the deer out so they can be shot.

Great, I'm thinking, I'll be waiting in case they chase a few deer over to my place. The next day we were ready. We took our spots. I picked out a stump to sit on. I looked to my neighbor's place. That's when I saw them four black bears headed my way. They were in a line running fast. They looked like a black line weaving through the woods. They were heading straight for me. I jumped up shouting and waving my arms, but they kept coming. Then I shot over their heads. Three turned off and went around me. The forth kept coming. I lowered my gun and placed the sights on her chest. I was slowly squeezing the trigger when she turned. I was glad I didn't have to kill her. She was a big sow. The other three bears, I think, were her cubs, though they good size. I paced off where she turned. I was fifteen paces. She could have gotten me if she wanted to. I went back to the cabin in a ball of sweat. Took a shot of whiskey to calm my nerves. It's a story I like to tell.

The first deer I shot, I was seventeen. I used a 7.65 bolt action Argentine First World War army rifle. I bought a box of shells. After I sighted my gun, I had only four shells left. Dad would not buy me any more. He said four shells is enough to shoot a deer. We lived by the philosophy that you only get one shot, so make it count. It was one of them cold winters. I started a fire and put my feet in the fire. I was so cold I was shaking. I was standing near the fire when I saw a deer a 150 yards off. I was on this hill overlooking Little Rat Lake. The deer was coming out of the woods, crossing the lake to a little out shoot of cat tails. I had my gun sighted for a hundred yards, so I raised the elevated sight one click. I fingered I'd click for fifty yards. When the deer was running, he made a kinda rocking motion. I waited for his shoulders to come up and fired my gun. He went into that clump of cattails and never came out. I walked down there and spotted blood where I first shot him. I walked over to the cattails and saw him lying there. I yelled and fired a shot to see if he would get up. There he stayed, so I looked him over, and he had one bullet hole in his neck. Here he was, my first eight-point buck.

About that time, this huge guy came out of the woods and said I shot his deer. I told him there is only one bullet hole in him and I put it there. He said he didn't shoot it, but he has been trailing him for two miles. He was a cussing man with a big red nose. He said, "Aren't you going to gut him out?"

I said I didn't have a knife, so he threw me his. Then I told him I didn't know how to gut a deer out.

"You mean to say you shot my deer and now you want me to gut him out? I'll do it, but I'm keeping the heart and liver." So he gutted the deer out, cussing all the time while gutting. When he was done, he took the heart and liver and walked away. When my guys came back, I told them what happened, then they helped me get the deer out of the woods. My brother-in-law owned a bar, and I was sitting in a booth. When I heard that big guy come in the bar, he was still cussing about that deer. I crunched down in the booth, hoping He would not see me. My brother-in-law called me over and said, "Meet my brother, Wally."

xlix

They were pulling a joke on me. Wally was a nice guy. This is not the end of the story. The next day, I had only two bullets left for the 7.65. Everyone decided I should take the .410 shotgun because it had six shells. I didn't like it because it had a limited distance or kill range. I took it anyway. I ended up in the same spot that I shot the eight-pointer. It was a little warmer then yesterday, so I climbed a tree and sat in a crotch about eight feet up. Must have been there a half hour when three does came right under the tree. I picked the biggest doe, lowered my gun. There was no aiming involved. I just put it between her shoulder blades and pulled the trigger. The doe was so close there was powder burns on her hair. When she jumped up, she pushed the gun into my face. I ended up getting a black eye. When I gutted her out, she didn't have a heart. I blew the heart completely out of her. And my black eye was an invitation to tell a story. I was proud. My dad was proud. I brag about that hunting season every chance I get. I guess I have always been lucky at deer hunting, except with a bow and arrow. I tried bow hunting for ten years and never got a deer. Every year I had my shot and always missed.

One time I went into the woods with nine arrows and came out with one arrow. I shot at eight deer and missed them all. I remember I was scouting this area. I parked my car and walked about twenty yards up this farm road. It came to a clearing, and there in this field stood a doe eating grass. I went back to the car and got my bow. When I got back, the deer was still standing there twenty yards from me in a field. I took my shot. My arrow hit a twig the size of a soda straw. The twig had a v branch. The arrow hit the v and went straight up in the air. The doe ran away. The arrow came down about where she was standing. I took this as an omen and gave up bow hunting.

Alaska

Drove up to Alaska July 1985. It was a bucket list thing for me. I wanted to go there before I was too old to enjoy the adventure. I bought new tires for the trip, some of the best tires Kmart had to offer. There was a lot of gravel on that Alaskan Highway. The campers had mettle mesh wrapped around them to protect their headlights and windows. Sometimes we had to travel twenty miles in a convoy because of the road construction.

When I got home, I had to replace all my tires. Luckily they were under warranty. The tire guy said he never seen anything like it on new tires. Stopping to see all the sights, it took us six days to get there. I was with my two sons: Tommy, 14, and Chris, 10. We camped all the way. I rented a room in Anchorage so we could do our laundry, take showers, and sleep on beds. Our main goal was to get to Homer about two hundred miles away so we could do some halibut fishing. When we got to Anchorage, the streets had rows and rows of furriers and pond shops. I went into a pond shop and saw shelves of cameras.

I said, "Hey, where did you get all them cameras?"

The owner said, "The natives take them when the tourist leave their cars unlocked."

I said, "Boys, it's time to go."

In Alaska, they have the largest seaport in the nation. The planes are tied up to the dock like boats. We left for Homer to check out charter prices; they were kinda pricey I remember seeing some cheaper prices on the way to Homer. We drove back sixty miles and saw a sign that said it had charters fifty dollars cheaper per person. It was a bar-restaurant place. I walked into the bar and said, "I wanted to rent a charter."

I paid the bartender.

He said, "Be here at nine in the morning."

I thought it was kinda late. The next day the skipper came out to meet us. He looked like a hippie, and maybe he had been partying all night. He said we start out later because we were closer to where the fish were. He said the charters out of Homer had to drive two and a half hours to get to this spot. He said, "They have too many people on their charters, and most likely you won't get a fish."

I think we fished four hours and got our limit. We threw anything back under twenty pounds. The biggest we got was sixty-four pounds. Tommy got that one. He was all worn-out by the time we got him aboard. When the fish gets close to the boat, you shoot him with a .22 rifle. He said if the fish flops around, it can break your leg. When we got back, we had someone clean our fish for a nominal fee.

We did a little salmon fishing while we were there. They had a lot of billboards offering charters. I stopped into one place to see about a charter. The man in charge said he could put us on an island, and we could fish all night for twenty-five dollars. He would pick us up in the morning. So we got our tent and cooler, and off we went.

It never gets dark in Alaska in July. He dropped us off on a chunk of land between two streams, said, "I will see you in the morning."

We caught some small salmon, butterflied them, and cooked them over a fire. Now this is how it should be. We were enjoying ourselves when we saw two guys fishing across the stream. They had shotguns with belts full of shells.

I said, "Are you hunting?"

He said, "There's a lot of bears in the area. This is for protection."

I didn't like the sound of that. Here I am stuck on an island with two kids till morning. After the guys left, I thought, *How am I going to protect myself if a bear comes?*

We didn't have any firewood to keep the fire going. I looked in my tackle box and found a fillet knife to protect myself with. On this island, there were large ferns ten to twelve feet high. The distance between them created large archways, like cathedral archways. The ferns were like a big wall obstructing my view. The kids went into the tent and fell asleep. It was hot and humid. I was sweating as I stood guard to protect my kids. It was about two in the morning when I heard a twig snap. And off in the distance, I saw one of them big ferns move. I'm thinking, *It's a bear.*

In a few more minutes, another fern move. No sense waking up the kids. We're all going to die anyway. In the meantime, the shaking was getting closer. The river is running white because of the volcanic ash. There's no place to run. The ferns very close to us are shaking. I got my knife, ready to fight. Sweat is running in my eyes. My shirt is sopping wet. Now the last fern is shaking. Out steps a blind porcupine. He walked right into the tent, turned around, and went right back into the fem.

My gosh, what a relief. I could have kissed the guy when he picked us up in the morning. Now when we headed home, we had 120 pounds of fish. We had to put dry ice in the coolers to keep the fish fresh. We had a couple of them Styrofoam coolers. One cracked and leaked fish juice all over the back seat. My car smelled like a fish cannery.

Now all the parks in British Columbia have these large steel buildings that one puts there trash in. On these buildings are large claw marks from bears. We camped in one of these parks. As we lay in the tent, I could smell the fish. I figured if I can smell the fish, so could the bears. We put all the coolers in the steel buildings, but the car still smelled like fish. We drove forty miles to the nearest town and slept under a streetlight.

Snakes

I took the boys out for a walk; exercise is good for your health. We must have been a mile from the house. We were walking in this field when I spotted this garden snake. It was the spring of that year, and the snakes were out sunning themselves. The snakes were all around, so I got a bag and started showing the boys how not to be afraid of snakes. I showed them how to pick the snakes up, to put their fingers behind the head tight enough so they wouldn't get away and soft enough so you wouldn't hurt them. We all had our turn, and the boys were having a good time. We must have had a dozen snakes in the bag. It was kinda cool watching them all slither in the bag. We brought them home and put them on the doorstep. And we started playing catch with the baseball. All of a sudden, we heard a terrible scream. The wife looked in the bag and almost had a heart attack. Upon the wife's insistence, I was persuaded to take the snakes back. I don't know what I was thinking, but you can bet I will never do that again.

Florida

It must have been 1959. We sold the bar for twenty thousand dollars. We were the richest people around. We packed up our things and were going to move to Florida. Ma had a sister that lived in Miami. We were going to live there too.

On the way to Florida, we saw some strange things. We were in the deep South and stopped at a restaurant. They had a drinking fountain attached to the side of the building with ice-cooled running water. Brother Jim and I ran over and started drinking the water. A policeman came over and picked me up and said, "That's the black boys' drinking fountain. If you want a drink of water, you go into the restaurant and ask for a glass of water."

It didn't make sense to me. I would rather have had that ice cold water running out of that faucet. There were a few other things that didn't make sense. Once we got lost and made a wrong turn. It was night out. It was a black town. We stopped at a stop-and-go light, and the black people started pounding on our car. I guess we weren't supposed to be there. We didn't know about discrimination.

When we got to Florida, it was cool, with all that ocean to swim in. First time for us to swim in saltwater. One can float a lot easier in saltwater. They even had outdoor showers so you could wash the salt off. I guess we weren't very smart. We bought a winter trailer in a tropical climate. Small windows and high humidity made sleeping difficult. They had common restrooms and showers in the trailer court.

At night the ground would be covered with cockroaches. In the morning you could see where you walked because of the dead roaches. At night when one made a crunching sound when they walked. We didn't have ask why. In the morning, we had to shake out our shoes because of scorpions and other insects. There were some good things. I remember we could go to a show house for ten bottle caps, and things were relatively cheap. Pop was a nickel; so was popcorn.

The school we went to spoke mostly Spanish. I remember the school didn't have any windows or screens; it was open air. We had little lizards running around the classroom, up on the ceilings, on the walls. The urinals in the boys' room were flush with the ground, and in the morning there would be scorpions trapped in the urinals. Me, Jim, and Jean got to school late so they put us by ourselves There was only two weeks of school left.

Dad use to like to take a nip or two out of the bottle. One day while driving, he hit a mail truck. That's a federal offense. He got thirty days on the chain gang and lost his driver's license. He had to wear a striped suit and leg chains. They made him cut grass along the roads in the Everglades; it was hot, and there was no shade. He said he killed a lot of snakes. We used to bring him lunch and cold water. When Dad did his time, we sold everything and left the state. Dad's Minnesota driver's license was still valid.

We went to California on the way back to Minnesota. Mother's sister-in-law lived there. We visited her. Then we went Disneyland; it cost about twenty dollars apiece back then to go to Disneyland. I don't think they were as big as they are now. Still we had fun going on the rides. I think we spent almost a whole day there. After that we went Capistrano. They say the swallows always come back to Capistrano the same time every year. You can set your watch by it. There are mud nest everywhere—on bridges clefts, houses. There's a lot of them.

Finally it time to head back to Minnesota. Good to be back and see old friends. When we went to visit Uncle Tony, I noticed a mud nest on the peak of his garage roof. I said to myself, "The swallows are back." So I climbed on the garage roof and stuck my finger in the nest hole to see if there were any baby birds. To my surprise, it was a mud wasp nest. A swarm came out of that nest like a cloud. I ran to Uncle Tony house swatting bees. Got stung on top of the head a few times. When I got in the house, there were twenty bees stuck to the screen door. I informed Uncle Tony that it was no swallow nest on his garage.

Bits and Pieces

I was thinking about a severely cold winter. I was up at my brother-in-law's place. He was a beekeeper. He had to move about twenty hives into this steel shed to get the bees out of the wind. I was a little hesitant; bees are not my friends. We were just about done moving them when the guy helping me dropped his end. A thousand bees were on me instantaneously. It was like I had on a beard of bees. They were trying to climb in my nose, my ears—anyplace to get out of the cold. I took my hand and brushed the bees off. They fell to the ground. It was twenty below.

As we got into the house and took our coats off, bees started flying all over the place. They came from under our collars and pockets, any nook and cranny where they could stay warm. I am not a beekeeper and found our little friends to be nerve rattling. They would be climbing on your coffee cup, maybe your arm or your ear. They were on the walls, the ceiling—everywhere. I was kinda thinking, What happens when you fall asleep? The next morning I didn't see any. They must have evaporated.

When we were kids, Mother had a unique way of controlling us when she went into the five- and-dime. She would tell us, "Here's a dime apiece. You can buy anything you want with this dime as long as you don't spend over it." There was a pretty good selection for a dime. You could buy a squirt gun, a jump rope, some jacks, candy, etc. This stopped us from asking for bigger things. And it taught us how to do math and about limitations.

I remember when I was young I could not tell one make of car from another. For instance, a Chevy from a Ford, what year the make was? One of my biggest fears was witnessing a crime and not being able to tell the police the make of the getaway car. The best I could do is tell them what color the car was.

Dad was a frugal man. When they went through the Depression, they were so poor that they didn't know there was a Depression. Dad used to straighten out bent nails so he could reuse them. Dad used to say, "Watch your nickels and dimes. The dollars will take care of themselves." When we used to go to the Goodwill store, Dad would say, "Put on your worn-out clothes, then if you see something, you want try and finagle the price down so we would get a 25 cent shirt for 15 cents." We did that with just about everything.

When we went to the farmers' market, we would go there late, just about closing time. We knew the farmers would want to get rid of their vegetables and not take them home. So we would get a large bag of corn, maybe two dozen ears for a quarters or maybe a large bag of tomatoes for 25 cents. Finagling was a way of life for my dad. It was a survival skill of its day.

I remember when my brother Bob bought his first house. He paid twenty thousand for it. My dad said to him, "Are you crazy. How are you going to pay for that place?" Dad was very upset and thought he raised a fool.

I remember once when cousin George came to visit. He loved my mother. He treated her like his mother. George's mother and father died at an early age. George was an orphan. Mother tried to adopt him but couldn't because we owned a bar. He always appreciated that she tried. Anyway George was visiting when a sidling salesman tried to sell Mother some siding.

The salesman put a piece of slate on the floor, stepped on it, and said, "See, you can't break this stuff."

George put a piece of newspaper on the floor, stepped on it, said, "You can't break this ether, but I'm not going to put this on the side of my house."

The salesman packed up and left.

Old Italian

I remember when I was a young (first house I bought), I bought this duplex next to this old Italian couple. The old man must have been eighty-five years old. We seem to have this unspoken tomato-growing contest. Every year I would put my tomatoes in weeks before him. Every year he would get bigger and better tomatoes than me. Finally I broke down.

I said to the old man, "How come every year I put my tomato plants in weeks before you and every year your tomatoes get bigger redder, and they ripen faster than mine?"

The old man said, "You're putting your tomatoes in too early. If the temperature drops below 35 degrees, it will stunt your plants. I noticed when buying tomato plants if the plants are purple, they are stunted, then they won't produce. Also, you should plant your plants up to the first two leaves so they can get a good root system."

I followed his advice and have had good luck with my tomatoes ever since. The old Italian died a few years later. Going to miss him.

I remember we had this mechanic at work, and he talked about what a wonderful place this was to work. He went to night school to become an electrician. After a while, he got his diploma. He was quite proud of himself and started to brag about himself, how he picked himself up by his bootstraps and had the gumption to succeed and make a better life for himself. He bragged so much he became obnoxious. He talked about how great he was and how great the company was.

One day he wired a million-dollar machine wrong and burned out a few key components, put the machine down for a few weeks. He cost the company millions of dollars. The company was now trying to fire him. (His tune changed.) Now he said this was a lousy place this was to work. He said now they're trying to fire him.

Loretta Lynn

In the early seventies my wife and I went to a Loretta Lynn concert. We had pretty close seats. It was intermission time. I told the wife I had to go to the restroom. In the restroom there was nobody there. When I came out, there was a policeman standing there. He pointed down the hall. I didn't want to go that way but went that way anyway. At

lxi

the end of the hallway stood another policeman pointing down some steps. So I went down the steps. There was another hallway. Halfway down the hallway was another policeman. He was pointing at a door with a big yellow star on it. I opened the door. It was Loretta Lynn's dressing room. Her fan club was there. When she came in the room, we all cheered. We gave her some kind of gift. She shook our hands, signed autographs. I took a few pictures. We screamed, "We love you." Then we left. When I got back to my seat, the wife asked what took me so long. I told her I was in Loretta Lynn's dressing room. She didn't believe me. A few weeks later, I got the film from my camera developed. There she was in the pictures. I made a believer out of the wife.

Mother said when she was a little girl, her mother took her and her brother and sister to the general store in a bigger city, maybe Devil's Lake? They bought this new stuff called Ice cream cone. They sat on the store stoop eating there ice cream. When they were done, Grandma collected the cones and wiped them off and returned them to the store owner.

Dad was born in 1901. He said the first car he ever seen, he chased for a mile to see where the horse was.

I remember I had a duplex. I lived in one side and rented out the other side. The people I rented to were a husband and wife and three kids, two girls and a boy. The father was an over the road trucker. It was Christmas day, and he was on the road. I bought the kids a little present and wished them a merry Christmas. About fifteen years later, I ran into one of the girls. She was all grown up with a babe of her own. She said, "I want to thank you for our Christmas presents. Did you know that they were the only presents we got that year?" Little did I know that a little kindness would have such a big effect. I felt a lump in my throat. Had I known they were so destitute, I would have done more.

I remember one day I stopped at this fancy restaurant. It was hot out, so I had me a cold beer. The place had a large oval bar. There was etched glass windows and etched glass on the doors. The crystal glass drinking glasses hung above the bar. Off to the side of the bar was a large dining area. This area had large dining tables with tablecloths and high-quality chairs. I was there about dinnertime. The place was bustling with activity, waiters and waitress running around, serving people quite a crowed. Don't think I could afford to eat there. Every table seemed to have a large bottle of wine. Some people brought their whole family there. They acted as if money meant nothing.

My crowd went to fast-food restaurants. A Whopper and fries would do just fine. Anyway, I was sitting at this large oval bar, just me and another guy. He was directly across from me, way on the other side of the bar. This women was hitting the guy on the shoulder, making a choking motion with her hands. The guy looked confused and yelled, "What do I do?"

I yelled, get behind her put your arms just below her rib cage and give a sharp thrust up. He did that and a large chunk of steak came flying out of her mouth. She gave him a big hug and thanked him many times before she left. I said to him, "You're a hero. If I had some money, I would buy you a beer." He said he had some money and would buy me a beer. And that is how a little intervention at the right time can save a life.

The Grocery Store

I was reminiscing. When my oldest son, Tommy, was little, he provided some interesting incidents. When he was in first grade, he learned to cross the street. They were taught to raise their hands and look both ways before crossing the street. We lived across the street from a grocery store. The time had come for Tommy to show off his newly acquired skills. His mother needed something from the store. She put $20 in an envelope, along with a note explaining what she needed. Tommy's mission was to go to the store under his mother's supervision and return with a few items and some change. Tommy was gleaming with pride. He stood tall and straight, looking both ways, raised his hands as he was taught; it was perfection, a textbook execution. He was consumed by his accomplishment and forgot his initial goal. And he then put the envelope in the mailbox on the corner. His smiling face gleamed as he looked for a congratulating well done. Instead his mother shrieked, "What the hell did you do?"

His mother had to wait two hours for the postman to get her envelope back. Twenty dollars was a lot of money back then, and Tommy would have to wait for some other time to shine.

Garbage Cans

Tommy, our oldest, had great confidence in his father. As most children his age, there is nothing his parents can't do. One day I came home from work and noticed the new garbage cans that I bought a few days earlier had big dents in them. I was enraged. I went into the house and screamed, "If I catch the garbage man denting them new cans, I'm going to punch him in the nose!"

A few days later, I was lying on the couch. The window was open a crack. I heard Tommy talking. He said, "If you dent them cans again, my dad's going to punch you in the nose."

I peeked out the window, and there stood two of the biggest garbage men I have ever seen in my life. One of the garbage men took the dented cans and pounded the dents out with his fists. He said to Tommy, "How's that?

Tommy told him that it was okay.

I sat on the couch imagining those big guys pounding on my head the way they pounded on them cans. When Tommy came in the house, I had to explain to him that what he hears in the house should not be repeated outside the house. That day, Tommy learned that some things should remain private. And I learned some things should not be said in front of kids.

Gun Cleaning

When I was young, about ten years old, my older brother had a civil war era rifle. It had a hexagon barrel and a chrome finish. It sure was pretty. Now my dad had this old Stevenson bolt action 22. It was old, and it had a dull finish. I didn't know about chrome back then. I thought my brother's gun was shiny because of polishing, so I got me some sandpaper and sanded all the bluing off my dad's gun. No matter how much I polished that gun, I could not get it to shine like my brother's gun. Well, I polished the best I could. I couldn't wait for my dad to get home from work so I could show him how I cleaned his gun. I told him I had a surprise for him and ran and got the gun. Dad looked at me and said, "What did you do?"

Then he explained bluing on a gun stopped it from rusting and that it was supposed to look that way. He said chrome was just for show and I wouldn't want to take a shiny gun in the woods it would scare all the animals away. I was surprised he didn't yell at me. I think he had the gun reblued. We used to go out on Saturdays and shoot tin cans for target practices. We put a lot of boxes of shells through that old gun.

PONDERINGS

A Book of Poetry

Contents

Knickknacks 73
The Pastor's Bird..75
Emancipated Woman 77
Arlington..78
Grandma's Place..79
Early Springtime[1]...81
Highway to Nowhere...83
The Butcher Man..84
A Puppet's Life..86
Old Man...87
When I Became a Millionaire..89
The Neighbor's Cat..91
The Cat Speaks...93
A Reflection..95
Robin Redbreast..97
Our Turn..99
It's the Loneliness I Can't Stand...................................100
Discipline..103

---

[1] "Early Springtime" was published in *The Metropolitan*, Metropolitan State University, Minnesota.

Clever Fellow...105
The Park...107
The Last Broken Dream...110
Winter's Death...112
The Pollywog..113
Long Tree Love² 114
Soldier Boy..115
Hunting Season...117
Proud Old Pillar...119
The Paper Game..121
House in the Wilderness 123
Familiar Ground...125
Like a Moth to a Flame..127
The Hanging Tree..129
Crystal Town 132
Backwards 134
Southern Wing..136
Politics and Industry 137
Unknown Man..138
Victims and Evangelists..140
Minnesota Winter and an Ode to Spring...................141
Conquests..143
Souls' Harbor..144
The Single Girl..146
The Monster Beast 148
Disorientated..149
A Book on Yonder Shelf...151
Fifty Miles and I'll Be Home......................................153
The Music Machine...155

---

² "Long Tree Love" was published in the anthology *At Days End* by the National Library of Poetry.

Dodging the Arrow	157
Pompous Idolatry	159
Anybody	160
Shadows	161
Sidelines	163
I'll Sleep Good Tonight	164
The Bank at the Edge of the Slums	166
The Thought	168
The Silent People	169
One More Time	170
Time	172
The Story of the Squirrel	174
Greed	176
Special Note	177
Just Put Yourself to Bed	178
Bill	179
Fall	181
Geese	182
Pseudo Virtue	183
The Hypocrite and the Pagan	184
Gossip	185
Hypocrite	186
Exposed	187
The City	188
Share	189
Burnt Out	190
Recluse	191
What a Curse to Be a Man	192
The Poet	193
Dear Lord Thank You	195
Photo Index	211

Knickknacks

Shelves and shelves and shelves and shelves
Of hundreds of knickknacks lay
Perhaps they're in order
Perhaps in disarray

Probably they're some memories
Of some eventful days
Perhaps, maybe
This I cannot say

Little things of rats and mice
Cats and dogs and bells and dice
Figurines of clowns and bums
Ballerinas and ducks and swans

They never stop, but go on and on
I would like to see, perhaps or chance
An earthquake come and make them dance
Then fall upon a concrete floor

And shatter them to nothing more
And maybe take this vacant space
With the knickknacks gone
Without a trace

And hang a picture thereabout
Of some countryside with barn and house
Or maybe a Rembrandt or Monet
Or maybe a sunset on some bay perhaps

The Pastor's Bird

A little bird sat cold and still frozen upon
his perch And his little lifeless body
fooled all those at the church

My, all the birdseed
that was strewn about the ground
With a little marble birdbath
so he could splash around

The pastor had a birdhouse
built and researched and designed
And everything was measured
so the hole was just his size

Then painted, primed, and ready so,
when the bird was inclined
He could put up residence
and keep the elements outside

And at the blessing ceremony
the choir sang so fine
All the children joined along
It made the pastor cry

Ah, what a precious moment
with everything sublime
And the little bird, dead on his
perch, didn't seem to mind

Emancipated Woman

You're an emancipated woman
    your life is now your own
Now you control your destiny
    though you must live alone
Now you have your freedom
    spread your wings and soar
Give to yourself the things you missed
    though you deserve much more
The shackles have been broken
    from the chains that held you
down You tried your best to make it work
    now you've been given grounds
To break that bond of loyalty
    and the vow you made yourself
You were the glue that held on to
    a dream and nothing else

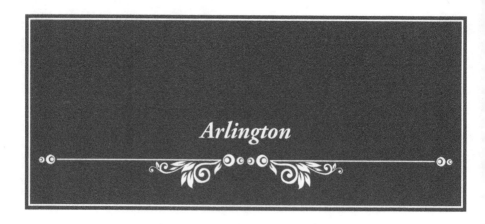

Arlington

The graves lay, one by one,
neatly in their rows
There's something about uniformity
that's soothing to the soul

The markers all look the same
white marble cut to size
Captains next to privates
and sergeants there they lie

Rank makes no distinction
there's no race behind the name
Just torn and tattered bodies
and wreaths upon the graves

My, what an exclusive club
that's bound by bond in strife
That strangers are all brothers
in death much more than life

Grandma's Place

The sun shone through the tattered lace
It filled the room with its warm embrace
An elegance in golden hue
Had hid the age like it was new

The dome-shaped lampshade spoke the truth.
Of grand old ladies in their youth
The lampstand stood as it was placed
The same as now as yesterday

Plush velvet drapes with sash and cord
The sun had aged and badly worn
The fabric of its eminence
Though its grandeur still was evident

An oval rug adorned the floor
Like a tapestry and still much more
The old stuffed chair stood stout and gray
Its doilies spoke of yesterday

Speak to me, oh, squeaky floor
As you have done long years before
When Grandma bought these things as new
When I was a child in my youth

Early Springtime

I went to the park in the early springtime
And gazed upon a grassy knoll
A shower kissed by northern winds
Had changed the raindrops into snow

Somehow, I became a witness
The snowflakes were so big and bold
That spring seemed to have lost its purpose
To heat the ground and make things grow

I watched the snowflakes fall in clusters
Making it hard for all to see
The last assault that they could muster
Before they meet their destiny

The robin stood quite bewildered
But the tulip shoots appeared to know
Winter is passed, there's no harm in her
We get the snow, but not the cold

The snowflakes seemed to melt on contact
On everything they grabbed ahold
They're only here for just a moment
Nature dictates that they must go

What a pleasure in the springtime
What an eyeful to behold
To see the contrast and the beauty
As I watched the wonderment unfold

Highway to Nowhere

The road was wide and well traveled too
    The trees had been cleared for an unobstructed view
The carrion eaters were all in their place
    Eating the roadkill till there wasn't a trace
And the turtle that was, is no more to be
    Ending the line of his family tree
And the squirrel lay there, he tried as he might,
    The cars came faster than his vision of sight
And the field mouse, possum, and raccoon were there,
    Birds became victims and even the deer
This once was a paradise and the animals roamed free
    When this stretch of the highway was acres of trees
Oh, uncountable cars, where do you roam
    Multitudes and multitudes, where do you go
Off to the horizon and soon out of sight
    On a highway to nowhere you just took a life

The Butcher Man

I had talked to the butcher man
    for a choice cut of meat
He had bloodstains on his clothing
    He had bloodstains on his feet

His hands looked thick from labor
    His eyes were filled with pride
He knew his job and did it well
    as he welcomed me inside

His knives looked new and shiny
    they lay neatly in a row
The band saw seemed well kept and clean
    the grinders seemed to glow

The display case shows he knows his craft
        the pork chops lay straight and lean
A better man is hard to find
        He keeps his shop so clean

But late at night when the shop is closed
        and the shades are all pulled down
In the back room there's activity
        and a high-pitched squealy sound

Who am I to guess his work
        and how the animals die
The soul stirs from just the thought
        It's better him than I

And as the family gathers
        as the call for us to eat
Bow your head and thank the Lord
        and please pass me the meat

A Puppet's Life

The puppet how he loved to dance
Though his steps were not his own
And how he loved to sing his songs
And he never sang alone

My, what a handsome lad
He had a striking pose
His antics made the children laugh
He wore the best of clothes

And he never lost a battle
And he vanquished all the foes
And he always killed the dragon
And brought the maiden home

And in the mighty castle
Where the maiden stayed
They lived happily ever after
Then they were put away

Old Man

The old man said, as he hung his head
With a tremble you see in the old
In my formidable years, I was a man to be feared
I was rash, big mouthed, and bold

But years have tempered the spirit
Fire has died in the soul
A cool breeze now chills the body
I stay inside to get out of the cold

And a smart mouth now seems threatening
The young folks have grown too bold
And old bones break too easy
And the body now moves to slow

And the ache in the bones bring misery
Now a shuffle instead of a stride
The distance has no horizon
For weakness has set in the eyes

So I'll take your respect or your pity
Or whatever it takes to get by
Till the Lord finds it is fitting
To take my soul, when it is time

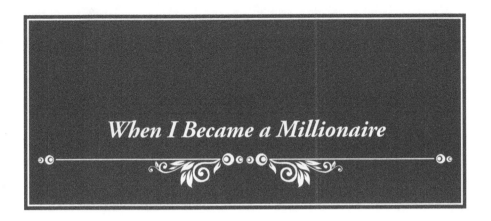

When I Became a Millionaire

When I became a millionaire
flowers were cast at my feet
My friends became many, the
women were all so sweet

And every day was sunny and every
day complete
Being popular with everyone to
go anywhere I please

Who are these begging masses
who grabble at my feet?
To think that I once knew them
hardly makes sense to me

To run around with tattered clothes
and beat-up tennis shoes
To talk about the rent and such
to sing about the blues

It must have been a terrible dream
to think I was one of them
Thank God for the lottery
and all my wealthy friends

The Neighbor's Cat

It was I who assumed such responsibility
As the neighbor handed me his key
He said, "Walk the dog and feed the cat.
In a week or so, I'll be back.

"The cat is sick and mostly lays.
By the flower bed, there's a fresh dug grave
If the worst should come to pass
Place her there in a gunnysack.

"We'll say some prayers when we get back."

A day or so had come to pass.
I did my chores as I was asked
The food dish lay on the floor.
The water bowl would take no more.
Where's the cat? I implored.

I sought her in the living room.
And on the couch and on the chest.
I sought her in the kitchen.
And everywhere, I guess.

Now upstairs to check the beds.
And there, to my surprise.
The top step on the stairwell
Is where the kitty lies.

I saw she wasn't moving
So with a gentle kick
She made a solid thumping sound
She was solid as a brick

And though I'm not a doctor
Nor do I ever pretend
She was dead as a doorknob
With rigor mortis setting in

So I placed her in a gunnysack
And laid her in her grave
Packed solid ground around her
And there she lies today

The Cat Speaks

I was gently napping
When I heard a gentle tapping
Something strange was happening
Something that I never felt before

When I went to sleep, the sky was sunny
Then someone stuck me in this gunny
This gunnysack and nothing more
As I woke from my slumber

The crushing ground sounds like thunder
How can I get out from under
Before I'm buried even more?
Stop the shoveling, I am pleading

From the lack of air, I'm hardly breathing
Who could do this deed? I'm screaming.
Is it a dream and nothing more?

With dirt in my eyes, I'm hardly seeing
I can hardly hear, my ears are bleeding
I grab for life, but life is fleeing
Is this what death has in store?

Now the sound is getting fainter
And I feel no more pain here
Maybe I'll just sleep a little more

A Reflection

When I was a child I loved to play
I'd imagine a mountain and climb it all day
Sinbad the sailor or maybe John Wayne
We'd fight all the Indians out on the range

I'd find me a forest old Davy Crockett and me
An old vacant lot with a few scrawny trees
And I'd play for hours, never kept track of the time
Anything could be done in this world of mine

If we had any enemies, thousands of them fell
Or maybe we'd scare them with an old rebel yell
We'd draw our swords and attack all the hills
Hand-to-hand combat, kill or be killed

Many a time I was shot in the side
And at the last moment help would arrive
A brave bunch, my friends and I
A message from the Alamo and away we would ride

Yes, the days went quickly
And got lost in the past
And only just now
Did I take the time to reflect

A treasure house of memories are stored in my mind
Waiting to be opened when I find the time

Robin Redbreast

Hello, Mr. Robin, glad to see your face
Welcome home, good fellow
How you made my day

I've been waiting for your arrival
As the snow melts away
As the geese are headed northward
As the spring brings the rain

And now it's official
Summer's on the way
As I wake up to your morning call
As you greet the sun each day

It's you who fills the silence
And keeps the bugs at bay
And your red breast brings me color
In my garden dark and gray

Your dance is amusing
It looks more like a prance
You cock your head from side to side
As almost in a trance

Then you run around hastily
And stop on a dime
Then spear the ground deliberately
For the treasures you will find

A worm for all your effort
To you it's quite a prize
The bounty from this rich black earth
Will help you to provide

For you a brand-new family
In the old apple tree
Just as did last summer
As you kept me company

Our Turn

Gray overcast, silhouetted by black gray trees
Each tree's tentacles reaching to the heavens,
as to wrap itself around life.
Each branch cries out, when is it our turn?
Each root drinking from the puddles formed
by the large drops of rain.
The now visible green shoots ebbing their way
through the rich blanket of nutrients.
Eating on the rotting decay of yesterday's glory.
Thus announcing, we have arrived.
Awake, brothers and sisters.
Have not the robins declared it?
Have you not heard the cardinal's song?
The inevitable is about to happen.
The long slumber is over.
Awake, all things
Awake, for winters harshness is over
It is now our turn.

It's the Loneliness I Can't Stand

The covers lay
    undisturbed
The unwashed glass
    the dirty shirt

The unopened mail
    lying about
The only one in
    the only one out

Dust gathered
    on the windowsill
No one to complain
    about a spill

Fresh-born ideas
    with no one to share
To be kept in seclusion
    as if they weren't there

There, the sound of silence
    hurts the ears
The unbridled imagination
    in the shadows bring fear

In this silence
    the phone never rings
One never hears laughter
    or the discussion of things

The radio plays
    another sad tune
Another shuttle launch
    on its way to the moon

And the world keeps turning
    and the choirs sing their hymns
Nobody cares
    they forgot about him

Then one day
    in the paper it read
A man in his apartment
    alone, was found dead

A gun in his hand
    aimed at his head
No mistake it was suicide
    the coroner said

Found in a note
    written in a shaky hand
The world is okay
    it's the loneliness I can't stand

Discipline

Lady, what are you doing?
My mind inside me shouts
This child you're protecting
Is a monster without doubt

He lacks any manners
And he has a viper's tongue
If he were a child of mine
I'd never call him son

I saw him smoking yesterday
And he runs with the pack
He owns everything that's not nailed down
And you'll never get it back

You should hear his vocabulary
It's still ringing in my ears
A four-letter onslaught
I haven't heard in years

How can you sit so pompous
With that monster you call son
How can you be blinded
To the damage that he's done

And when he gets in trouble
You run to his side
Backing his convictions
Justice being denied

Somewhere in the future
In not so very long
I'll hear your cries of anguish
Where did I go wrong

Clever Fellow

I am a very clever fellow
I'm careful in what I say
I'll lead you on just enough
so you can take it either way

I will build up your hope
and let you wait in despair
As you trod upon this shaky ground
wondering if I care

Time is not an element for me anymore
I've passed the stage of the younger age
I'm not as susceptible as before

And you as ripened fruit
left drying on the tree
You've made your plans
on shifting sand
You haven't consulted me

Let me tell you something
it wasn't all my fault
I gazed upon your composition
there were danger signs sticking out

I've put you under a microscope
I've observed you under different lights
I saw the web you were spinning
As your thoughts reeled out of sight

I'll never meet your expectations
And a white knight I'll never be
Crusading for your worldly wants
Is not the life for me

So I'll keep leading you on
As you think you're leading me
Till you grow up or I humble down
Whatever the case may be

The Park

I heard your voice on the wind.
I heard you call my name.
An image of you darted through my mind,
    and it caused me to smile.
I could smell the perfume at the nap of your neck as you
    tipped your head and your hair fell to one side.
The image faded all too fast, as it awakened
    other thoughts of you.
A crow cried out his loneliness (there was no reply).
Fall is here, and the leaves are changing their colors.
The sky is gray, and the ground is wet. A
    slight chill could be noted in the air.
Dusk was settling in the park. The deserted
    benches where lovers sit took
on a ring of sadness. It was as if all the
    lovers in the world were gone.

The vitality of spring and summer have passed.
    Now trees settle into their dormancy
As flowers wilt and die, one cannot help
    dwell on the passing of time.
The fall's bareness and coldness allows for a
    certain clarity. There's no distraction of
    color in the blandness of nature's gray.
In the stillness of fall's quelled activity, the barren
    picnic tables, the deserted playground, where
    the wind dances amongst empty swings.
Nature tends to isolate pleasures, causing one's
    thought to turn inward. Nature grants the
    stillness of serenity without distraction.
A time to take inventory. A time to lay
    plans. A time for privacy.
In this privacy, evasive questions manifest themselves,
    along with the profoundness of wrenching truths.
Question of life and death, the shortness of time allotted,
    and what part one plays in the scheme of things.
With all gaudy precepts gone, along with the
    delusion of instilled happiness,
One finds humility.
Like nature stripped of all her splendor. All charades are
    put aside. Life is broken down to black and white.
The primary necessity for existence is love.
    With it, a myriad of emotions.
And a reason to go on living.

Darkness had overtaken the park. Along
     with darkness came its insecurities.
The thought of safety and comfort had overwhelmed
     the moment. As my thoughts turned homeward.
Supper, Television, and You.

The Last Broken Dream

A friend of mine felt inclined
to dispel the things I know
He said in trust, with a laughing lust
and a smile so big and bold

There's no tooth fairy that comes at night
and buys your teeth, so bright and white
It's always been your mom and dad
and all these years you've been had

Another year had come to pass
Christmas time was here at last
When there came another friend
who would shatter my hopes from here on end

There's no Santa Claus, he said with delight
I asked my mom if he was right
I saw the sadness in her eyes
she felt no joy at the dream's demise

The Easter bunny came and went
by now it was evident
That all these things that brought me joy
were lies they told to girls and boys

The Sandman no longer came
nor did Jack Frost write on the windowpane
The moon's not made of cheese
nor do we mate for life, just like geese

Winter's Death

Winter, killer of the flowers
Has March loosened your grip?
Your friend, the shadow, still speaks of your might
But the sun laughs at your stubbornness

Winter, your glory the snow has become slushy and dirty
The fine embroidery of your work is becoming unraveled
The budding trees speak of your death
on the sun's heated breath

Winter, your time is becoming short
Your wrath is now limited to the night
and the nights are getting shorter
The shadows will no longer protect you

Winter, spring comes and with her she brings life
And all things new
And you, the killer of flowers, will soon be forgotten

The Pollywog

The pollywog outgrew his pond
metamorphosis complete
Where his wiggly tail was
he now grew some feet

And now he breathed air with new formed lungs
and how the air was sweet
Instead of digesting mucky marsh
he now had bugs to eat

And out of the darkness grew the light
so plain for all to see
That if pollywogs can turn to frogs
It's the same with you and me

Long Tree Love

Here the mighty elm tree stands
reaching to the sky
A heart was carved upon its branch
to proclaim to passersby
That love was here many years ago
and that a girl and guy
Had found this place to call their own
so they could spend some time
Together they would make a pledge
together they would try
To meet the future hand in hand
and that's the reason why
You will find this proclamation
twenty feet up the tree
With Grandpa and Grandma's initials
as father told it to me.

It was you who died, oh soldier boy
for a cause so noble and true
With the flag unfurled and the drummers roll
you did what you had to do

You lined up for your death charge
and in your heart you knew
Your letter said that you'd be dead
before the day was through

In an unknown field, in an unknown place
the force of the battle grew
And every man would tend his spot
as he was instructed to

The glitter of the bayonets
the glare of the rising sun
Many a man would lay in state
before this day was done

And for you with so much courage
that proved you were a man
They have no name just an unmarked grave
and a used-up battle plan

Hunting Season

The leaves have fallen
Now there's nowhere to hide.
Every movement is detected.
Crunching and thrashing can be heard.
Every step rings out an alarm.
The animals of the forest are tense
Their forage for food, before winter, becomes urgent.
They must pause for every sound,
any intruder is untimely.
There's danger in the air, for it's hunting season.

Leaves cover the ground, like a crunchy carpet.
An alarm system devised by nature
It crunches when walked upon.
The noise can be heard for hundreds of yards.
Every animal makes its own distinct sound.
The heavier animals crack twigs and branches

The annoying clumsiness of man
as he bangs and stumbles
through the woods is all too identifiable.
If, by chance, a human, the stalker
of prey, were to pause and
remain motionless for an hour or so.
The animals would come out of hiding.
They would then become vulnerable
to the wishes of the hunter.
Then it's a simple matter of pick and choose.

An animal's speed and grace is no match for a bullet.
An abundance of any species brings the wrath of man.
Man's cunning and cleverness is stored in books.
He can kill beyond the range of detection.
Every animal has been catalogued,
data has been compiled as to
the animals' habitat, mating rituals, and vulnerabilities.
There are no secrets.

These creatures can be taken at will, and they are.
Their only protection is the same species that hunt them.
Quotas, limits, and regulated seasons.
We must allow them time to replenish, to repopulate.
This way, we can kill again.
There are many trophies to be had.

Proud Old Pillar

My what a wonderful old wrinkled man
He once tilled the soil
and worked the land

He did his work without complaint
Through the burning sun
through the pouring rain

And on and on
his hands served him well
From cutting trees
to digging wells

They built the house
and picked the fruit
Worked the grinder
that sharpened tools

Fed the cattle
picked the corn
Helped baby calves
so they'd get born

The sun burnt hard
upon his back
His shirt was bleached
from all his sweat

And now he rests
in the rocking chair
Speak up loudly
he can hardly hear

And treat him kindly
he earned his place
This proud old pillar
of the human race

The Paper Game

I don't want to play it anymore, I've grown weary of it.
It was fun at first, now it's the opposite
It was a game that became abused, shuffled then reshuffled
And they changed the rules.
You never get to be the banker, the penalties are real.
Someone smarter than me is playing the game.
And I think their cheating at the deal.
But they're so pleasant, how could it be possible?
Wolf in sheep clothing, with "let me
help you" written on their sleeves.
The game take advantage of the fool, laugh
at his innocence and gullibility.
Take till he can't play anymore.
As each player thinks he knows his own limitations,
He still becomes swallowed up beyond his capabilities.
The hidden clause that magnifies
itself when brought to light.

You didn't read the rules
As lawyers hover over their hosts, like
buzzards circling their prey
Ready to devour the unfortunate losers.
Each will extract their pound of flesh
till they're clean to the bone.
Being unsatisfied, they'll look for more.
A game, lying like an iceberg, treacherous, alluring.
Inviting the inquisitive to all its entrapments.
Have I got a deal for you, sign here.

House in the Wilderness

I built a house in the wilderness
an encroachment on sacred ground
Purity in its primal state
no paths or glass was found
The foliage was so lush and thick
it blinded one to see
The natural lay of the land
as to retain its privacy
To wander far from the house and car
would make a tender foot believe
Without a doubt, there's no way out
and that they met their destiny
Where north is south and east is west
and the moss surrounds the trees
Where a canopy obscures the sun
no landmarks can be seen

Where mosquitoes swarm and the ticks adorn
the underbrush and the weeds
Where coyotes howl at the moon
and the deer and the bear roam free
Nature is as nature does
and she does as she please
Savage to the unprepared
and merciless in her deeds
But if one were to bend to her whims and ways
and to trust in God and luck
Learn her secrets and hold them dear
abide by her rules and such
You can overcome your primal fears
and the thought of being alone
Then enjoy the peace and serenity
and call this place your home

Familiar Ground

Ah, this old familiar ground
I've been here before It's caused me a lot of
hardship so I'm cautious all the more

And though you may be innocent
as I thought one time before
My gullibility leaves me vulnerable
my stupidity even more

So for me I've chosen
to go through life alone
Than suffer another mortal wound
that could crush my heart and soul

I don't have to be compatible
or give more than I can take
I don't have to be accountable
for the mistakes that you might make

And when you become irrational
that holds true to the gender form
It won't be me who's victimized
once bitten is forewarned

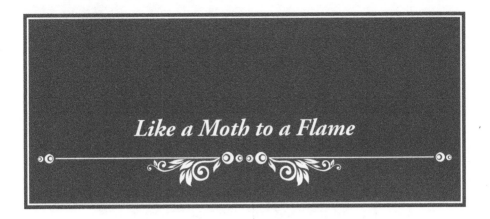

Like a Moth to a Flame

I was led just like a moth
To your fragrance and your charm
And I was filled with wander-lust
To hold you in my arms

Why does the flame burn so bright?
I have no will at all
The charm's been set by nature's way
And I can't resist the call

I've made a hazardous journey
Mostly by chance
The road's been filled by treachery
As I fluttered in my dance

I've seen the praying mantis
The spider and the wasp
I've seen the carnage strewn about
As I ascertain the cost

All is dared for one brief chance
One moment to aspire
Then I will reach new lofty heights
Then dive into the fire

The Hanging Tree

Way out back
where the grass grows tall
Where the wood tick flourishes
where the bullfrog calls

There stands a big rock
and a rotting tree
That's home to the squirrels
and the bumblebees

The tree was tall
with a branchy beam
The old folks
called it the hanging tree

And late at night
when the barn owl calls
When the night hawk screeches
and the lone wolf howls

One can see clearly
on a moon-filled night
When the wind just whispers
and the dew's just right

An old black buggy
with a black horse to match
A silhouetted figure
with a slight hunchback

With ragged clothes
and an old dried wreath
With a half-bowed head
and some rosary beads

She'll grab her mouth
and let out with a scream
As if she saw something
that should remain unseen
Then she'll disappear
horse and buggy and all
And all that remains
is the night bird's call

There's never tracks
that one can see
As you look about the ground
by the hanging tree

So if you go out
on a moon-filled night
where the wind just whispers
and the dew's just right

And if you dare go back
where the grass grows tall
Where the wood tick flourishes
where the bullfrog calls

There might be something
you just might see
By the one lone rock
and the hanging tree

And if you see something
tell the doctor so
and that I'm not crazy
so they'll let me go

Crystal Town

The sun has set on Crystal town
from sea to shining sea
Now all things that could have been
are left to destiny

Darkness reigns through hallowed halls
who recites the creed?
There's nothing left, no stone unturned
to feed that monster greed

Who can feed upon himself
if cut will they not bleed?
Who can turn his head at will,
and pretend he doesn't see?

The reaper reaps what the sower sowed
the scythe has cut it clean
The orphans and the widows starve
there's nothing left to glean

See, said I, with a mournful cry
the prophecies foretold
When death becomes a welcome thought
so God can claim the soul.

Backwards

I bent over backward
just so I could see
I bent over backwards
are you the one for me?

I didn't flinch or yell out a word
when you hurt my pride
I tried to understand your ways
to reason every side

And I went backwards
I put up with your laziness
I thought it was just a spell
I didn't know you couldn't cook
and there's nothing you do well

And I went backwards

You never get up at dawn
to feel the morning dew
Or go camping by firelight
the ground's too hard for you

So I went backwards

When I tell a joke or two
you never understand
And if it comes to pleasing me
I don't think you ever can

Yup, backwards

Here's some aspirin for your headache
and some thought for your brain
If by chance you catch someone
forgive my refrain

He'll be backwards back—wards

Southern Wing

To the oldest part of the hospital
To the southern wing he goes
Where the sun always shines
He'll spend the rest of his time
Which won't be very long, I'm told

The man got tired of living
The man is very, very old
His acquaintance of past
Have long since gone
His life has come to a close

And there you'll find no visitors
Only the hospital knows
Make him comfortable as you can
This old ancient man
And send a minister to look after his soul

Politics and Industry

Words were bent by heated tongues
The forge glowed an eerie hue
The brightness blinded everyone
Except for just a few

Palms were creased by
Industrial grease
And the bearings were all lubed
And its intent was never meant
And easily misconstrued

I am afraid we've been betrayed
For somehow, I feel used
When a job well done, said everyone
I read it in the news

Unknown Man

What can be said
to a man who has failed
Who has tried everything
but never avails

What can be said
to a man from the start
Who gave a hundred percent
Who gave from the heart

Like a man's feet, that's on ice
an untimely slip
That shatters his hopes
his dreams slip from his grip

Like a brainwashed man
beaten and broke
Dismayed, disillusioned
sometimes beyond hope

He keeps being pulled down
by the gravity of things
No hope for tomorrow
or what the future will bring

He finally submits
He finally succumbs
He lives down by the tracks
He lives with the bums

Yes, every city has them
You'll see them dressed in rags
Their food's in a bottle
in a little brown bag

To hard-hearted children
these men become prey
They hide under bridges
to stay out of the way

And when they come out
it's by twos or threes
There's safety in numbers for men such as these

And when they die
The city will claim
A wayward soul
with no home or no name

Victims and Evangelists

They searched for hope so they could cope, and they
searched near and far. Confused and dazed,
lost in a maze, beat up and battle scarred
As they approached the noise, I heard
the boys like a circus barker's call
This is it, it's tailor fit, and you can have it all
With great pretense they did convince, the crowd was
wall to wall
When following their Judas goat, the butcher got them all
I ran in fear, eyes filled with tears,
I saw the slaughtered fall
They were victims of their ignorance
to which they were at fault

Minnesota Winter and an Ode to Spring

The rigors and turmoil of winter have reached its zenith. We have survived thus far.
The mind and the soul cries for spring. The accumulation of snow has been devastating. The cattle and the wild animals suffer. Old folks become home bound. Schools close periodically due to the extreme wind chill. Skin can freeze in thirty seconds at -60 below. Cabin fever and short hours of daylight make everyone depressed. We count the days till spring.

Who But You, Spring

Who but you can lengthen the day,
    smite the snow, melt it away
Who but you can bud the trees
bring with you, the birds and bees

Who but you can wake the bears
    bring forth the flowers, sweeten up the air
Wash away the dirt and grime
and dry it out by summertime

Who but you can clear the lakes, free
    them from their icy fate
Bring forth shoots and grassy beds for
    baby fawns to rest their heads
Who but you can fill the creeks
    that make the homes for ducks and geese
Fill the swamps and fill the bogs, turn
    tadpoles into toads and frogs
Make mating birds fluff their wings
    and late at night, make the cricket sing
Now Mother Nature works in stride and
    sometimes shows her ugly side
We've been through this many times before now,
    our bones are old, and our joints are sore
So now I lumber off to bed
    the forecaster predicts bad days ahead
But I lay in my bed consoled
    knowing there's an end to the ice and snow

Conquests

You grab then acquire
then satisfy the urge
Lose interest in your conquest
seek new trials in you search

Something new is on the horizon
where's your commitment now
Promises to be broken
no obligation to them vows

Look at the ruin
and the carnage you left behind
Each one of them a treasure
and now you change your mind

Souls' Harbor

You'll see them at the missions
their faces tell it all
Poverty knows no boundaries, though,
the poor are first to fall

Joe lost his job at the foundry
Bill lost his at the mill
Margaret had a drinking problem
Jack was mentally ill

They all came together
with the same need in their lives
To find shelter from the elements
and the food they need to survive

Once life was sunny
it wasn't always this way
They grew up like most children
then something went astray

You can sit and listen for hours
of the hardships in their lives
And shed a tear and share their fear
who knows where they'll be tomorrow night

Some say they're lucky
they weren't turned away
Others say they were lucky
they had food to eat today

They found Steven yesterday
frozen in his sleep
Huddled in someone's doorway
trying to find some heat

If it wasn't for the missions
who would really care?
Souls harbor is a sanctuary
Thank God that they are there

The Single Girl

What are you up to, now that it's Saturday night?
You've been waiting for that someone
And tonight might be the night
You spent all your morning shopping for new clothes
They're revealing, they're daring
You look irresistible to behold
A trip to the beautician, you've got the latest style
It captured all your highlights
It was well worth the while
Your tan paid off this summer, it accents your clothes
Your teeth were never whiter, and oh that perfect nose
And that hour in front of the mirror,
to compliment your eyes
They sparkle like diamonds, they look twice their size
And oh, those perfect cheek bones on that solemn face
And oh, those innocent puckered
lips seem never out of place

Now the hour is drawing, it's almost time to go
To release to the unsuspecting horde, this beautiful abode
Well, you reached your destination,
could this bar be the place
Where is Prince Charming, as you glance at every face?
The hours pass quickly searching through the night
You can have anyone for the choosing
But you never found Mr. Right
Yes, you got a lot of attention, and that was your aim
You had a lot of fun tonight, you drove the men insane
But deep down inside your hollow,
There's this little gnawing pain
For that special someone you hope to meet one day
Well, it's an hour past midnight,
something about pumpkin shell
Your crystals losing all its shine, your magic lost its spell
So you muster up some courage,
and you say it's time to go
Like a reoccurring nightmare again you leave alone
Back to your apartment, time to make new plans
Maybe next weekend you'll find that special man.

Strategies are not the same
> *the old exchanged for new*

Policies that govern us
> *are now no longer true*

Adapt or die the battle cry
> *or haven't you heard the news*

On solid ground, you've been phased down
> *they cut the crew in two*

Instead of eight you now have four
Instead of four now two
Instead of two you just have one
> *and you're the lucky few*

Yes, corporate greed, that monster beast
> *has sold a soul or two*

You've been displaced, you're out of date
> *there's no room for the likes of you*

No tears of grief from the monster beast
> *with the profit margin down*

There's no remorse, the plan's on course
> *we have to shut her down*

Disorientated

I've been told so many things
about this and that
Politics and religion
there's so many views to be had

Sometimes, I get so turned around
I don't know where I am
Just when I think I've made a stand
I'm turned around again

How I envy a man with conviction
be it right or wrong
To pursue his goals in earnest
He's even honest when he's wrong

To run around without direction
like a leaf in the wind
To be tossed around mercilessly
a victim of every whim

Well, give me your information
But here's where I take a stand
Till I sort out this terrible mess
if I ever can

And please, don't point your finger
or condemn me to hell
For I'm not for you to judge
and it's probably just as well

A Book on Yonder Shelf

A book I found on yonder shelf
raised my curiosity
Thoughts of men long past gone
was written in poetry

I read the verses one by one
with a tear and shaky hand
For those old poets had written down
the essence of man

They told of joy and great loss
They told of war and death
They gave their philosophy of life
And what they thought was best

They tugged on your heartstrings
with their golden pens
were pondered long and hard
to make them rhyme and blend

The words they used to describe their thoughts
ring with antiquity
The book I held within my palm
was written at the turn of the century

Fifty Miles and I'll Be Home

This old Ford, she squeaks and shakes
She's rusted through and needs new brakes
And I'm on this road alone
50 miles and I'll be home

The snap and pop of cracking trees
The sound they make when they start to freeze
Ah, this cold can chill the bone
40 miles and I'll be home

The snow, she drifts across the road
She's making drifts, where she grabs ahold
I don't know how I got so bold
30 more miles and I'll be home

The sun she went behind the hill
It's hard to see, but I can make it still
Though my feet are numb and cold
20 more miles and I'll be home

This old car don't drive to fast
It will be close, I'm short on gas
The heaters broke, my nose is froze
10 more miles and I'll be home

Off in the distance I can see the lights
I told my mom I'd be home tonight
Now everything will be all right
And I'll be home for Christmas

The Music Machine

The fat cat drove up in his music machine
To sell dreams by the gram
The dancers had rainbows in their eyes
And make-believe on their minds
They compromised many tomorrows
For one today
A trade-off, one's life for a million stars
Jimmy Cool procured some monitory gain
A predator that feeds on unlocked doors
And a boldness that crosses all rationality
What's up?
A handshake that ends palms down
An exchange of misery
That feeds the music machine
And keeps the music machine alive
Life as it was now ceased to exist

The transformation was complete
The dark room exploded into a million stars
As Jimmy once again met God
With the sorrow that cruised through his veins
With rage under his breath
With freedom on his mind

Dodging the Arrow

He was filled with pride, it was in his eyes
He held himself quite erect
He filled everyone's anticipation
He adjusted to every request

Oh, how great to be in the lamplight
And have everyone looking at you
And to cover any inadequacy
Direct them to Mr. two

The farther you point down the ladder
The higher up you seem A stepping stone
on someone's failures Can make you feel
supreme

But be careful climbing that ladder
Clouds can obstruct your view
You can't see how to be humble
And you can't see who's looking at you

Just when you think you're invincible
Something will happen to you
Someone like you is down there lurking
And is ready to step upon you

To capitalize on your mistakes
Waiting for you to make the wrong move
Now it's you who can dodge the arrows
While reflecting on how many you threw

Twisting the circumstances Making
false what's really true They'll
magnify small problems Until they
overcome you

If you have to set an example
In everything that you do
That's exactly what you'll be When
your replaced by Mr. Two

Pompous Idolatry

Give me a rainy gloomy day, Where
the lust and shine is gone
Where everything balances, Where
the gaudy plumage is
camouflaged in the shadows. Where
all colors are suppressed,
Its magnitude diminished by fate's hand.
These monuments, created for
adoration, made at the expense
of your souls and the hardships
imposed by your greed.
Ask a hungry man if he cares?
Your creations have created false
realities, leading onlookers
to believe all is well.

Anybody

I've been looking
and you have too
We've lowered our standards
both me and you

To fill that gap
now we've grown old
No one's perfect
like we've been told

And we're tired of searching
and it's time to rest
To take that chance
before our deaths

What a change from perfect
to someone to anyone
And that's how it is
when you're lonesome

Shadows

It's the nighttime of my life
reflective figures against the wall
Without any substance
still, reflections of it all

Does a shadow have emotions?
if not, why did I see one cry
He was holding his head in anguish
as the night went slowly by

The shadow reached out to touch someone
but his hand was never felt
A mimicry of affection
a mimicry of oneself

Lost forever
in the recesses of the mind
Tiptoeing quietly
appearing from time to time

A flash of a vision
too quick to recognize
Always present, always lurking
but never to materialize

I don't want to be this shadow
if you hear me, please understand
You hold the key to set me free
help this imprisoned man

Sidelines

You're tired of the fast life
You're tired of you know who
You road it out to its last mile
now a change is due

You deserve something better
so you'd like to start anew
Totally forget the past
and all its claims on you

So you put on your white dress
divorce you know who
Go to church on Sunday
and become a teetotaler too

So you sit on the sidelines
and watch a game or two
Get amused at life's complexities
and be glad it isn't you

I'll Sleep Good Tonight

Ah, the plushest carpet
Emerald green are the walls
And blue is the ceiling
And fragrance fills the halls

You can have your mansions
Your nightclubs and your bars
And you can keep your city
With its crime and all its cars

And I will take the countryside
Where nature still is free
Where the bears walk the forest
And the trees sway in the breeze

Where nighttime takes its place
The only light the moon and stars
The only sound are frogs and crickets
The only heat from a warm bonfire

Mesmerize me reaching flames
Ember missiles burning bright
A few hours more, I implore
Until I sleep good tonight

The Bank at the Edge of the Slums

Confusion, old, cold, his chair made of
quicksand and his lips blistered from
things you want to hear.
The invisible bowl of posterity washed down
with the sour milk of human kindness.
I've seen it, written on throwaway
towels down at the bank.
Where the fat man washed his hands.
Where the skinny people waited in lines.
Where the Joneses kept up with the Joneses.
Where the children cried unattended in the new cars.
What's that smell, the innocent one cried, as bloodsuckers
crawled on a paper chain attached to his vein.
As he waited in the loan officer's chair.
There the computer dissected the applicant,
exposing the broken dreams. *Welcome* was written
on the icing that covered the moldy cake.

Take another piece, they told the poor man,
as they led him to the back door, so could
vomit in the sewer that was his home.
From the back door one could see the slums.
There an eerie darkness from the lawyer's
shadow touched every house.
Where the radio blares, unemployment
is down two percent
Where children play amongst the broken
glass, with free cheese stuck to their
faces and powdered milk on their lips.
There the pusher says to the children,
I have a new game we can play.
But first you must sell your stolen bicycles.
There a blind policeman was talking
to a slut on the street comer.
And did not see the hoodlums rob the old
lady's house next to the church.
Where graffiti builds invisible fences and prophets
get their visions from little brown bags.
Thus, they shut the door quickly. For the sunlight
hurt their conscience and the cries hurt their ears.
As they continued to provide a much-
needed service for the community.

The Thought

The thought ricocheted from neuron to neuron trying to
Find its way out of the prison that held it.
And as it touched any and all, it exploded
into a word, yet another word.
And it screamed, write me down before I get lost
in the maze from whence I came. Write me down
for I have the complexity and the uniqueness of a
snowflake. And I shall never be duplicated again.
Write me down or all will be lost. And I will be
just another flicker of light in the millions and
billions of light that bring about you brilliance.
Write me down and you can claim the
prize and I can claim immortality.

The Silent People

I sat and watched the silent people
They hardly made a sound
If you didn't take the time to notice them
You wouldn't know that they're around

They blend into the background
They're very hard to see
They never cause a distraction
Or impose on you or me

They never ask for nothing
They get on by themselves
They take the strife dealt out by life
Without uttering a sound

Who are these silent people?
Who can they be?
Some underground organization?
They're not people like you and me

One More Time

I went down to my favorite bar
To see it one more time
All those people that I knew
And all those friends of mine

Jimmy was staggering
And Mike had a few
Julie put the make on Tom
And everybody knew

The jukebox was playing
It almost hurt the ears
The old man at the bar
Was aged beyond his years

The ashtrays were smoldering
And smoke filled the air
Rent was due tomorrow
And no one seemed to care

It was just like a play
Everyone did their part
They brought it to perfection
They played it from the heart

But nobody seemed to care
Because everybody knew
We'd all be back tomorrow
To stop and have a few

Time

The sand trickles fast in the hourglass of time.
As each granule falls, no matter how fine.
It plummets through a tapered neck.
That monitors the flow to an even trek.
In this constant, even flow.
In single file, we'll watch them go.
On and on, as we watch awhile
Their being consumed into a pile.
A monument to time gone past.
And even now it's hard to grasp
You can't recover what has gone
In our allotted measured time.
Each moment counts, no matter how fine
To a constant even flow
In an overall prospective, you would see it so
As thousands upon thousands before us went
Each had its purpose for which it was sent
Till the present forms the past.

As each event becomes the last
Till we take our place, there will be no denial
As we stop and rest a while
Till we form our monument
That shows the purpose for which we're sent

The Story of the Squirrel

The little red squirrel lived near the edge of the woods. He was quite content with his style of living. He had his own territory staked out, his own perimeters set. He foraged for food, eating nuts, pinecones, seeds, and most things that squirrels eat. Every once in a while, he would chase away an invading squirrel out of his territory, but that was to be expected. For this was life in the woods

One day a farmer decided to feed the deer who also lived in the woods. The farmer put a large pile of corn right in the middle of the little squirrel's territory. The little squirrel was ecstatic. This is more food than the little squirrel had seen in his entire life. Instinct told him he should bury this food and save it for harder times, but other squirrels had also seen the corn. And the little squirrel had to chase them away. Birds had seen the corn and wanted to eat it. Now the little squirrel not only had to bury his corn, he also had to chase away would-be thieves. All day long the little squirrel ran around chasing other squirrels and birds. And had very little time to bury his corn.

One day the farmer decided to watch the deer eat his corn, but all he saw was the little squirrel running back and forth. From what the farmer could see, the little squirrel was stealing all the corn, thus making the poor deer starve.

My, what a greedy little squirrel, thought the farmer. *That he would not share his food with the other animals.*

The farmer decided to shoot the squirrel. He would then return harmony to the woods, for every animal should have his share of the food. Thus the farmer shot the squirrel, and harmony returned to the woods, for a few hours anyway. For another little squirrel found this territory unclaimed. He would claim it for himself, and the same process would start all over again. Now the new squirrel would have to protect his new territory with its pile of corn. And he too would spend most of his time chasing away birds and other squirrels.

For this is the squirrel's nature; he cannot stop doing what he is doing, even though he is destroying himself. He could not see that greed was wearing him out. And that too much of a good thing is not always good.

Greed

It was big and round and it blocked the sun
it cast its shadow on everyone
It seemed to devour everything it seen
it kept on rolling and it picked up speed

As fear and panic crossed the land
beyond comprehension to understand
Everyone was touched by this infernal thing
it created a vacuum and corrupted deeds

It left a blemish here and there
it left a stench that filled up the air
Its deceptive smile could entice
it polluted the innocent once or twice

It's gone for now, it'll be back again
it lurks in the souls of mortal men
And they call it greed

Special Note

The poem "The Neighbors Cat Number 12" was written about an event that happened to a friend of mine. I found the story a bit humorous in a sad sort of way, the friend being a gentle-hearted soul. I thought to pose the question, "Are you sure the cat was dead?"

The poem "The Cat Speaks Number 13" is a response from the cat as if he were alive. As a pun, I wrote it in the form of Edgar Allen Poe's "The Raven."

Just Put Yourself to Bed

The day has passed quickly
It's time to head home
Past the church, down the block
Where I live alone

It's quiet when you're by yourself
You get the paper read
And if you want to sleep an hour
You just put yourself to bed

Bill

Bill was a second cousin of my neighbor. He was somewhat of a backyard philosopher. Bill had some pretty interesting views on the subject of happiness. Bill says, "There's no such thing as love."

And he should know, he's been married four times.

Bill says, "Those optimistic lifetime believers go to their graves believing lies. They spend their entire lives thinking their happy. How sad."

Bill spends all his time being sad for all the happy people. Because they don't realize how miserable they really are.

Bill says, "I can't believe how gullible these people really are. You see them all the time, smiling, driving their new cars, smiling at weddings, not realizing they just made a forty-year commitment to a lifestyle they can't afford. Disneyland was made for these people. It's sad to see them perpetuate the myth of happiness. A make-believe world brought to reality, which was a lie to start out with. Eighty percent of these people should be living in tents. They'd be much happier, don't you know?"

Bill says, "If they had an old beater of a car like I do, they'd really be happy."

Bill said, reluctantly, yes, he would trade his old car and his old house for somebody's new ones just to give them a shot at real happiness. And once they find out what real happiness is, they can be sad too.

Bill says, "I'm no brain surgeon, but most of these people are maladjusted, ill-informed and duped into buying a dream and also living that dream."

Bill said, "I tried to convince my last four wives of this. Unfortunately they all lacked the ability to grasp what I was trying to say. They all wanted too many new things so they could be falsely happy. When all the time, I gave them the opportunity to be righteously happy."

"Well, you know what they say about a prophet in his own country."

"I rest my case."

Fall

It was a cold north wind that was coming in
it was raw and it stung the nose
Animals were putting on their winter fur
people were putting on more clothes

The hunters were busy polishing their guns
the archer strung up his bow
The harvest was done and fall had begun
the jack-o'-lantern lit up and glowed

The leaves had all changed their colors
the smell of firewood hung in the air
Daylight hours had shortened their time
and there were flocks of birds in the air

Softly silhouetted against the sky
in v formation they go flying by
If you listen closely you can hear them call
It's a honking sound that tells of fall

When the air is crisp and clear
and you feel a chill
and the cold nips the ears
You can see them clearly cross a harvest moon
over clean-cut fields to a wind song tune

Pseudo Virtue

It was you who cast down the gauntlet
And would defend it to the very end
An idea that lacked foundation
To the delight of all your friends

And chivalry, though well intended
lacks innocence, though you pretend
And the battle now ensuing
Was a lie since it began

Could there be alternative motives
That could make one to transcend
To carry a pledge to battle
And fight it to the very end?

And the name was changed for concealment
On the surface one must contend
That all was well with the morals
And virtue would win in the end

The Hypocrite and the Pagan

I put on my deception
a fantasy we share
You believe that I'm believing
as my stench fills up the air

Disillusioning your trust, in the future
you might have ventured there
In the day he is righteous
at night he doesn't care

And you say "Where is Eden"
"or God if I dare"
"I've seen his saintly servant
and I know he doesn't care"

"Get away from me, chameleon
I've seen your colors change
There never was a God
and all of you are insane"

Gossip

This, whisper, whisper, whisper
This gossip and charades
This planning and this scheming
Then anger filled with rage

You buzz around from bee to bee
There's a story to be told
As you mimic those around you
As gossip takes its toll

Once blown out of proportion
And spiced up for size
Its intent was never mentioned
With its truth immersed in lies

Hypocrite

On shelves you store your evils
out of sight and packed away
Ready to be pulled back out
when you don't feel in a saintly way

You keep these things about you
You're not finished with them yet
They served what you were after
and won your confidence

The roads well-worn and clearly marked
you gave up keeping score
The boundary line is fading
you can't distinguish it anymore

And as these things become interwoven
and matted all the more
You have become the prisoner
of all the evils you have stored

Exposed

On paper, my thoughts lay exposed and scattered
before you, uninhibited and naked, open to
your inspection, to probe and pick apart.
As you analyze my reasoning, as
we both touch familiar
ground. Your ax lays ready, you
are the executioner, you
are the judge, but I struck the first blow.
It was my fault for enticing you.
So then we both die,
I in my innocence and you in your integrity.

The City

I don't like the city
and all this urban sprawl
Houses upon houses
people, wall to wall

You'll have to drive an hour
to see the countryside
To enjoy its serenity
to enjoy its peace of mind

Concrete upon concrete
Buildings oh so tall
Silhouetted sunsets
monuments to the malls

Share

Won't you let me share your dream
this utopian fantasy you have
Something you find happiness in
the things that make you glad

I would like to know what brings you
pleasure so I can get some more for you
And maybe if there's a little left over
I could have a little bit too

Burnt Out

You're feeling fine, you blew your mind
But where is reality?
It's a high, but it's a lie
A dream world, a fantasy

There is no place you can escape
Without paying the penalty
And what you got
Your dead brain cells have bought
You're a zombie in the world of humanity

You've got no clique without your trick
That makes you Mr. Personality
Life is gray any other way
Your existence is a falsity

Recluse

I've become quite shy
somewhat of a recluse
Instead of addressing things straight on
I turn inward from the truth

Much like an ostrich
with his head stuck in the sand
Maybe my troubles will go away
and not come back again

What a Curse to Be a Man

A story about a mortal man
and the death that he did fear
Minutes turned to hours
and weeks had turned to years

In his torment and his anguish
he screamed throughout the land
What a fate to be had by all
what a curse to be a man

The Poet

It was he who took the simple thought
and turned it inside out
Then he studied all its secrets
and shook the thought about

Then he mixed it with a bunch of words
and tried to give it spin
So he could move the soul around
or whatever moves within

To the right would give you laughter
To the left would make you cry
Just to leave the thought alone
would simply let it die

Then he gave it rhyme and meter
as he studied every line
So he could please the reader
as he crept into your mind

Ah, to take you on his journey
on his magic ride
To give you thoughts to ponder
as you see things through his eyes

And he thanks you for your interest
And the time that you have spent
And he hopes he brought you pleasure
for that was his intent

Dear Lord Thank You

Dear Lord thank you for my gifts, my talents, my health. I've been granted riches greater than the great Kings of history. Did they have carpeting, large TVs, cable, heat at their fingertips, air conditioning in the hot summer running water, indoor plumbing. I have wonderful woman to take care of me. Two wonderful boys, two grandchildren, one great grandchild…grocery stores at our discretion. Fresh fruit in and out of season, three cars, two houses. Acreage A safe journey thru life, longevity. All things were possible thru you Oh lord. Employment my whole life. Thank you for my privileged existence and thy Love and the strength and logic to overcome my disability. Forgive my feeble attempt to sing you praise. THANK YOU.

Tom Platzer running the 1985 Twin City Marathon

GrandPa young boy in the middle he was 11 years old
—picture taken in 1882.

Teammate Of Thorpe's Dies Here

Dan Ryan's article.

Daniel Plante, Kalamazoo resident who was a teammate of the fabulous Jim Thorpe at Carlisle Institute, died Sunday afternoon at Borgess Hospital.

Plante, 65, of 322 Cooley St., played three years as a guard on the Carlisle Indian team that was led by the pile-driving running of Thorpe, voted the outstanding athlete of the half-century.

Survivors include two sons, Daniel Jr., of Kalamazoo, and Francis, a Trappist brother at an abbey in Kentucky, and a daughter, Mary, now Mother Mary St. John Vianney, at the Cardinal Hayes Convalescent Home, Mill Brook, N.Y.

Funeral services will be held Tuesday at 8:30 p.m. at St. Augustine Church. Burial will be in Mount Olivet Cemetery Wednesday morning at 9.

Uncle Danial played with Jim Thorpe at Carlisle Indian school in 1910.

one of Toms wood carvings

Toms All City picture top third from right

Uncle Louis and Uncle William 1st WW They stayed with the French people because they could speak French. One of them got shot in the foot and had to stay in a fox hole for three days till an ambulance could pick him up. The ambulance was full. So he had to hold on to the out side of the ambulance.

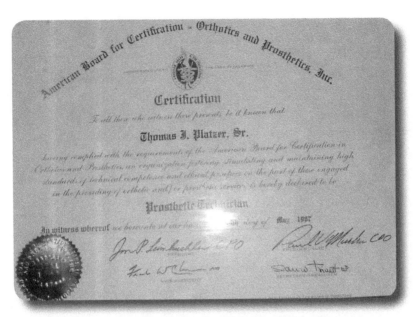

Prosthetic Certification

Twelve point buck

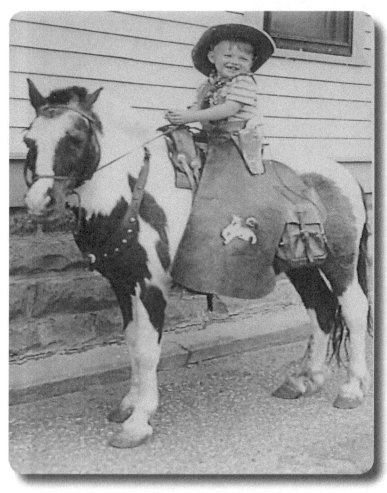

Tom on pony

Dad with Jim and Jean (twins) Me in the middle

Dad cavalry picture

Grandma and grandpa homestead picture

Tom's civil war carving

Dad's cavalry picture

Grandpa picture died 1936

Dad's cavalry picture

Jean Platzer: Homecoming 1966

Infant Child of a Cannon Ball Rancher is Missing.

Friday, about 1 o'clock in the afternoon, George Platzer of Hobson, about fifteen miles south of Mandan, lost his little girl, 2½ months old, on the prairie, and she has not yet been found.

It seems that Platzer's three children, aged five, four and about two years respectively, were playing around the ranch after the noonday meal. About 1 o'clock the two elder children came i and upon their mother asking where the youngest was, one said she was asleep and another that a man had carried her off in a wagon. Search was immediately commenced, and a posse of citizens have been hunting day and night ever since, but without result. A report is current that Pete Black Hawk, who was in custody in connection with the Spicer murders, offered to buy the child some time ago, and the parents firmly believe some Indians have stolen the child. In support of this theory they claim that the child had on a large cap belonging to its father, and if a wolf or coyote had carried it off the cap would surely have dropped somewhere.

Sub-Agent Wells is having a strict search made through the Indian camp for the missing child, but those familiar with the Indians scout the idea of their stealing a white child. There is intense excitement in the Hobson and Fort Rice neighborhoods and the

Grandpas brother had a child stolen by the Indians

Alaska fishing trip Halibut fishin

Dad in Indian outfit

Tom Indian identification card

Photo Index

1. Picture of auther Tom Platzer running the Twin City marathon 1985 on page 196

2. Grandfather—young boy center of picture my G-grandmother center on bottom—picture was taken in 1882 p 196

3. Article about uncle Daniel playing football with the great Jim Thorpe p 197 Carlyle Indian school

4. Duck wood carving by Tom Platzer p 198

5. All City Picture Pioneer Press—Mechanic Arts 1966 third on right- top p 199

6. Picture of uncles Louis and William Plante 1st World War p 200

7. Tom Platzer—Prosthetic Certification p 201

8. 12 point buck p 201

9. Tom Platzer on pony maybe 5yrs old p 202

10. Dad and kids Tom center Jim and Jean on ends Jim and Jean twins p 203

11. Robert Platzer—DAD 1st world war cavalry picture p 204

12. Grandma and Grandpa—home stead picture p 205

13. Author Tom Platzer Civil war relief carving p 205

14. 1st world war Calvary picture 3 subjects p 207

15. Calvary picture Dad p 207

16. Jean Platzer its her homecoming picture-1966 p 207

17. Grandpa picture died in 1936 p 206

18. Article about Great uncle George—one of his kids was kidnapped buy Indians p 208

19. Alaska fishing trip p 209

20. Dad in Indian outfit p 210

21. Anthers Indian card p 210

About the Author

Hi my name is Tom Platzer. I was born April 25, 1949, in Saint Paul, Minnesota. They say I was born with my umbilical cord wrapped around my neck. Maybe this accounts for my disability. They always said Minnesota was a few years behind the rest of the known world. When I was little, the world was changing at a fast pace. The street cars were leaving the scene. The Korean War had just ended. The milkman was still delivering milk on ice. As kids, we felt safe to go out and play by ourselves. One of the few cardinal rules was to be home by supper. All adults were addressed as Mr. and Mrs. My friend's parents didn't have first names. If we had any problems, we could ask any adult for help. This was the prevailing attitude till my early teens. The day of innocence was gone.

As I grew older, I began to see life with a new prospective. I learned not to trust the opinions of other people. Mother used to say you take everything you hear with a grain of salt. The world was changing fast. Microwave ovens, Color TVs. Men on the moon. Race Riots, Vietnam, John Kennedy assassinated. The Beatles; Wood stock; Bob Dylan; The Rolling Stones—everything was coming at a fast pace. And I believe everything is still coming at a fast pace. We have become desensitized, less shocked to atrocities. The news sensationalizes everything. We have become skeptical. The root core of our being has been shaken. We no longer know right from wrong. All these life experiences make us who we are. And our family values are imprinted on our subconscious minds.

"Since they show the work of the law is written in their hearts. Their conscience also bearing witness and their thoughts either accusing or defending them" (Rom. 2:15).

So, our conscience dictates our actions, and a weak conscience leads to bad decisions. Maybe my thoughts are just the ravings of an old man. Or maybe the world is becoming more lawless. We will just have to wait and see.

CPSIA information can be obtained
at www.ICGtesting.com
Printed in the USA
FFHW020630120819
54212618-59941FF